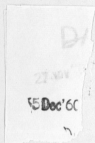

Management Policies
in
American Banks

Management Policies
in
American Banks

A Study Based on a Survey of the
Federal and State Supervisory Agencies

BY

HOMER J. LIVINGSTON

President, The First National Bank of Chicago
and
Past President, The American Bankers Association

Foreword by EDWARD E. BROWN
Chairman of the Board, The First National Bank of Chicago

HARPER & BROTHERS PUBLISHERS

NEW YORK

There is one responsibility of the banker which transcends every other banking obligation, and that is the responsibility to manage his bank with the highest degree of competency, so that the safety of the bank's deposits is assured.

CONTENTS

FOREWORD

BY EDWARD E. BROWN

Chairman of the Board, The First National Bank of Chicago

The American banking system is not only the center of the nation's financial institutions but it occupies a position of far-reaching importance in the business and industrial life of the nation. It is imperative, therefore, that bankers bring to their responsibilities the highest competence. In no segment of the American economy is sound management more important than in banking.

There is a constant need in banking literature for practical material which will assist bankers in the daily discharge of their management responsibilities. This study of the principles of bank management should be of value to every banker. The opinions and conclusions on bank management included in this book were obtained through answers to questionnaires, and through opinions expressed, by the state and national supervisory agencies, which cooperated on a nationwide basis.

With the help of these agencies, which annually examine thousands of banks over the country, a more comprehensive study has been obtained than would have been possible by an appraisal by one person of the management policies of the nation's banks.

The book discusses the major aspects of sound bank administration, and it presents a practical analysis of the strong and weak points of management.

It is my pleasure to commend the book and its objective of seeking to bring the highest degree of competence to the management of American banks.

... the replies in this book, together with some further elaboration on the subject of bank management. If this study of
managerial policies in American banks contains suggestions
that prove helpful to anyone in banking, it will in part reward
the many supervisory agencies who so generously have made
it possible.

Thomas I. Storrs

PREFACE

THE national and state supervisory agencies in the course
of examining the more than 14,000 banks under their respective jurisdictions have a unique opportunity to observe
the operations of American banks. The responsibilities of
these agencies permit them to review and evaluate critically
the management policies of banks of all sizes. From their
broad supervisory experience, these agencies are therefore in
a position to provide information of practical value on bank
management to bankers and to university faculty members
and students of banking.

In an effort to obtain this information and make it generally available, we prepared a comprehensive questionnaire
on the major aspects of bank management and submitted it
to all the state and national supervisory agencies. Forty-one
state supervisory agencies, the offices of the Board of Governors of the Federal Reserve System, the Comptroller of the
Currency, the Federal Deposit Insurance Corporation, the
Deputy Bank Examiner, Territory of Hawaii, and the Department of the Treasury, Commonwealth of Puerto Rico,
responded to the request for information.

The generous and thoughtful response of these agencies
to the questionnaire is greatly appreciated. Their extensive
answers to the questions, as well as the illustrations many
of the agencies included, prompted the decision to incorpo-

rate the replies in this book, together with some further elaboration of the subject of bank management. If this study of management policies in American banks contains suggestions that prove helpful to any of its readers, it will in part reward the many supervisory agencies who so unselfishly have made it possible.

HOMER J. LIVINGSTON

Management Policies
in
American Banks

THE BANKER'S FIRST RESPONSIBILITY

THE one responsibility of the banker which transcends every other banking obligation is the responsibility to safeguard the depositors' funds entrusted to his stewardship. That is the banker's first responsibility.

The confidence which the men and women of a community place in a bank can be fully rewarded only by conscientious and capable management. It cannot be repeated too frequently that there can never be any substitute for able management. Only by bringing superior management to his bank, and in no other way, can the banker properly meet the needs of his depositors, his community, and his stockholders.

There are at least eight significant aspects of bank management.

First, there is the obligation to provide adequate credit to the businessmen, consumers, and farmers of our nation.

Second, the banker must be skillful in the management of bond investments.

Third, the responsible banker must have a thorough knowledge of Government monetary and fiscal policies, Treasury debt management and the Federal Reserve System and their relationship to the entire banking system of 14,367[1] banks.

[1] Board of Governors of the Federal Reserve System *Annual Report,* Washington, 1954, p. 81.

Fourth, every banker must be painstakingly aware of the need for building bank capital accounts.

Fifth, good management necessitates a good auditing and control system in every bank.

Sixth, there must be carefully considered plans for selection and training of officers and employees, and for the development of competent successor management.

Seventh, to meet fully the requirements of banking leadership, the banker must have an intelligent understanding of world banking and financial problems.

Finally, bankers must be constantly aware of the vast economic and social implications of their banking activities. The manner in which bankers demonstrate farsighted economic and social vision will largely determine the tone and temper of public opinion regarding the banking system.

How well, then, do bankers discharge their responsibilities? Difficult, practical problems for which there are no ready-made solutions cross their desks every day. Do bankers become lost in the day-to-day routine and often fail to give their banks the firm policy direction for which they are clearly responsible? Each borrower, depositor, stockholder, and banker undoubtedly has his own answers to that question. However, there is one group which can evaluate the soundness and capacity of bank management throughout the country with unusually authoritative judgment. This group is the state and national supervisory agencies. These agencies have made constructive and indispensable contributions to the sound development of our national and state banking systems since the early days of American banking.

Year after year these agencies examine the 14,367 banks,

giving careful attention to the loan portfolios, the bond accounts, the capital accounts, and the auditing and accounting controls. They study the earnings and losses on loans and investments. They analyze the disposition of bank earnings in the payment of dividends, additions to reserves, and the building of capital accounts. Because of these studies a summary of their views on the strong and weak points of management should be revealing.

Consequently, we wrote to all the national and state supervisory agencies asking a great many questions on bank management. The response was excellent, and we are grateful for their generous cooperation. The survey includes agencies that examine almost every bank in the United States, Puerto Rico and Hawaii.

We asked each of them to give us the benefit of their views regarding bank management under a number of broad headings. A copy of the questionnaire on bank management is shown in Appendix A. We believe that this is the first time the views on bank management of the supervisory agencies over the United States have been brought into one study. This book is an attempt to summarize these views. These opinions reflect the examiners' long and comprehensive experience in examining banks. Their thoughtful and constructive observations merit our careful consideration.

ECONOMIC CHANGE AND THE EFFECT ON BANKING

There is everywhere today an increasing realization that the world has experienced economic, social, and political changes in recent years of far-reaching significance. In the

United States, the flow of world events and the gigantic forward strides of the American economy are compelling banks and businesses constantly to re-examine their policies and their objectives.

In order to measure properly the responsibilities of leadership in the banking system today, it is necessary to look briefly at the economic history of the United States since the turn of the century, and to see how the opportunity and the need for banking services have grown step-by-step with the nation's remarkable economic growth. In the rise of the national economy, we have not only one of the amazing chapters of our history, but also the foundation for the development of the nation's banking services in all their complex variety.

Let us look at a few of the areas that indicate how the need for banking services has grown and will continue to grow with the further expansion of business and industry in the years ahead. Some of the forces operating in the economy today are old, but some of them are entirely new. A hundred and one competing demands beat upon our desks each day, and often we tend to overlook, or we accept as commonplace, the forces which are making such significant changes in our economy. These changes are occurring each day so clearly, so significantly, and so unmistakably before our eyes that we fail to evaluate their importance. Yet, in the aggregate, these shifts in the American economy represent great changes in our dynamic society. If the banker is to measure his responsibilities and opportunities properly in the years ahead, he needs to understand the nature of these changes and the reasons for the economic expansion there is every reason to believe will occur during the next decade. He needs also to understand better the magnitude of the social and economic setting in which he may be rendering banking services in the future.

ECONOMIC GROWTH

Table 1 shows that the country's population has increased over 75 per cent from 1910 to 1954, home ownership has more than doubled during this period, and life insurance in force has increased from about $15 billion to over $333 billion.

TABLE 1

Year	Population[a] (*Thousands*)	Home[b] Ownership (*Thousands*)	Life Insurance[c] In Force (*$ Millions*)
1910	92,407	9,084	14,908
1920	106,466	10,867	40,540
1930	123,188	14,002	106,413
1940	132,122	15,195	115,530
1950	151,683	23,560	234,168
1954	162,414	24,900[d]	333,719

[a] From U. S. Department of Commerce, *Statistical Abstract of the United States*, 1955, p. 13.
[b] *Ibid.*, p. 782.
[c] Compiled from *Life Insurance Fact Book*, 1955, which draws data from the *Spectator Year Book* and the Institute of Life Insurance.
[d] *Federal Reserve Bulletin*, August 1955, p. 859.

Table 2 sets forth the growth in the nation's production, capital investment, national income and personal savings.

TABLE 2. GROSS NATIONAL PRODUCT AND SELECTED
COMPONENTS—BY DECADES
(Billions of Dollars)

Year	Gross National Product	Gross Private Domestic Investment	National Income	Personal Savings
1930	91.1	10.3	75.7	3.4
1940	100.6	13.2	81.6	4.2
1950	285.1	51.2	240.0	12.1
1954ᵃ	360.5	47.2	299.7	18.3

SOURCE: Economic Report of the President, 1955, years 1930-50.
ᵃ U. S. Department of Commerce, *Survey of Current Business.*

Gross national product (the total national output of goods and services annually) has increased nearly 300 per cent since 1930; gross private domestic investment (the sum of new construction and net flow into all inventories annually) has risen over 350 per cent; national income (the aggregate earnings of our people annually) shows a four-fold increase since 1930; and personal savings since 1930 have increased nearly six times.

Remarkable as these developments have been, the changes now on the horizon appear to be even greater. It is not an easy task to adjust our thinking to the vast changes which today dictate the direction and determine the development of the American economy. It is easier to follow the accepted routines and the inherited opinions of the past, but if history teaches anything, it teaches that constant change is the only certainty in the life and enterprise of a free society. When change stops, the enterprise and genius of a nation are dead.

In the coming decade we may experience economic ups and

downs. We do not have to be as optimistic as those who believe we shall never have another serious recession. However, many major sustaining factors in the economy strongly indicate that the nation's long-term economic trend is upward. Banking leadership adequate to meet the enlarged responsibilities resulting from a continued growth in the nation's economy is imperative.

POPULATION

One of the foremost single elements of change in the economic picture is the growth of the nation's population. Recent studies estimate that during the next ten years the population will increase approximately 2.5 million persons per year. At the end of 1950, there were more married couples and a larger proportion of our people married than ever before.

The growing population is creating shortages in many local facilities, and there is insistent demand that these conditions be remedied speedily. Almost every community has a need for increased school facilities. Based upon recent estimates, about $2 billion of additional school construction will be required annually over the next decade to take care of the accumulated backlog, to offset depreciation, and to take care of the increased enrollment. Hospital construction requirements are estimated to be $1 billion yearly. Public utilities are expected to reach an annual spending rate of more than $4 billion. Increasing capital outlays may be expected for a long time to come for highway construction. Whether or not a total of $50 billion or more for such expenditures in the next ten years is attained, it is certain that enormous sums will be spent to rebuild our highway system so that it will meet more adequately the needs of the continually increasing number of motor vehicles.

In recent years, there have been large expenditures for housing construction, and yet over 60 per cent of all homes today are over twenty years old, and 50 per cent of them are more than thirty years old. Large-scale modernization of existing homes seems inevitable. A number of cities must undertake great programs of rebuilding in order to eliminate slum areas.

MIDDLE INCOME FAMILIES

Of outstanding importance is the enormous increase in middle-income families—their tremendous growth numerically, their needs, and the opportunities they have opened up to American industry. We have a new kind of middle class, big, prosperous, and constantly expanding. Of an estimated 51 million family units in the United States in 1953, 18 million families, or about one out of every three, were in the $4000 to $7500 annual income group. This middle income group has more than tripled in both numbers and income since 1929.[2] This great class promises to become a decisive market for services of all kinds. The substantial increase in the relative and absolute number of families in the middle income brackets is one of the most important social changes in this generation. Income distribution has undergone revolutionary changes during the last twenty years. More families have more insurance, more income, and more wealth, and they have more need for bank services.

[2] Gilbert Burck and Sanford Parker, "The Changing American Market," *Fortune,* August 1953, pp. 98-105.

EDUCATION

Increased educational opportunities for our people also stimulate economic progress, which in turn generates an expansion of bank facilities. The growth of higher education in the United States has been phenomenal. During the last fifty years the number of students enrolled in private colleges and universities has multiplied seventeen times. More widespread education means steadily higher standards of living, more production, better homes, more use of credit.

Thirty-five million Americans in 1953 took part in adult education programs. But even with all our educational attainments, less than one-third of college-age young people are in school. The possibilities for expansion here are of great magnitude.

TECHNOLOGICAL RESEARCH

One of the fundamental forces in the economy is the rapidly expanding volume of scientific research. More than 5000 privately owned industrial organizations employ 250,000 scientists. There is a direct relationship between this work and the industrial output of the nation. For example, in the postwar period research has created at least three new major industries—petro-chemicals, electronics, and nuclear energy. In the next few years, industry should receive even greater stimulus from technological progress. In 1939, for instance, it was estimated that about one third of the number of persons employed had jobs that were based upon inventions, scientific discoveries, and technological developments. Today, it is estimated that possibly one-half of all employment in the United States is based upon products which come from scientific research laboratories.

The forces set in motion by modern technology and rising productivity are irresistible. They mean greater abundance, lower costs, price reductions, new products, new enterprises, and millions of new jobs. They mean large industries with a greater need for banking services. The driving force of our restless and expanding research serves not only to satisfy the wants of an increasing population but also to create new wants and higher standards.

A WORD ABOUT THE FUTURE

The American economy is dynamic in its technology and industrial output and in the wide distribution of income to the people. The Joint Committee on the Economic Report[3] has estimated that total output may increase approximately 50 per cent by 1965. They also estimate that business expenditures on plant and equipment may amount to about $60 billion per year by 1965, compared with $38 billion in 1954. Such growth would create a need for an accumulation of capital on a scale much larger than ever before. As businesses grow larger in number and in size,[4] traditional banking services will have to be expanded to accommodate the demands of business.

---

[3] Joint Committee on the Economic Report, *Potential Economic Growth of the United States During the Next Decade,* 1954, pp. 8 and 11.

[4] Total corporate assets have increased from $334 billion in 1930 to an estimated $722 billion in 1952. Total corporate earnings, after taxes, rose from $3.9 billion in 1930 to nearly $20 billion in 1952.

GROWTH OF BANKING

Has the banking industry kept pace with the nation's progress? The answer to this question is expressed more dramatically by statistics than by mere words. Table 3 illustrates the growth of the national banking system since 1790.

TABLE 3. TOTAL ASSETS, CAPITAL AND DEPOSITS—
ALL ACTIVE BANKS[a]
(*millions of dollars*)

Year	Total Assets	Total Capital	Total Deposits
1790	N.A.	2.5	N.A.
1800	N.A.	21	N.A.
1820	N.A.	102	31
1840	658	358	120
1860	1,000	422	310
1880	3,399	826	2,222
1900	10,786	1,907	8,513
1910	22,450	3,836	17,584
1920	52,828	5,954	41,725
1930	73,462	10,282	59,847
1940	80,214	8,325	71,154
1950	192,241	13,916	176,120
1954[b]	231,654	17,270	211,115

SOURCE: U. S. Department of Commerce, *Statistical Abstract of the United States*, 1955, p. 433, except for years 1790-1820 which are taken from Roy A. Foulke, *The Sinews of American Commerce*, Dun & Bradstreet, Inc., 1941, p. 386.

[a] All active banks in the United States and possessions including savings and private banks.

[b] *Federal Reserve Bulletin.*

The first commercial bank made its appearance shortly before the end of the Revolutionary War. By 1790, there were four banks whose capital totaled $2.5 million. By 1840, there were 901 banks with an aggregate capital of $358 million and total deposits of $120 million.

By 1880, there were over 3300 banks with a capitalization of $826 million, and total deposits of about $2.22 billion. By 1900, there were over 10,000 banks with a capitalization of almost $2 billion, and total deposits of $8.5 billion.

The banking system went through the severe money panic of 1907, and a distinguished American banker said of the banking system in March of that year, "I am in daily terror of something giving way under the strain." Call loans could not be obtained even with an interest rate of 125 per cent. And yet on December 31, 1910, the capital funds of the American banking system were up from $1.9 billion in 1900 to $3.8 billion, and deposits had increased from $8.5 billion to $17.6 billion.

On the night of December 31, 1910, no one in the banking system could have foreseen how our people were to be shaken out of their serenity in the next ten years. Before the end of 1920 the banks went through a business decline in 1913, the earth shaking impact of a great world war and a boom in 1919. And yet on December 31, 1920, the capital funds of the banking system had increased from $3.8 billion to $5.9 billion, and deposits were up from $17.6 billion to $41.7 billion in only ten years.

Fortunately, as 1920 closed, no banker could have anticipated all that would happen in the next ten years. In 1921, there was a severe depression, with 20,000 business failures, one-fifth of the people in manufacturing and transportation unemployed, one-third of those in coal mining and construction out of jobs, and wages down as much as 25 per cent to 50 per cent. There was tremendous industrial expansion in the 1920's, but at the same time there was an agricultural depression so severe that 471 banks failed in one state alone from 1922 to 1928, inclusive. Then came the collapse of the stock market boom in 1929. Gradually the lengthening shadow of a deep depression settled over the world. In the 1920's we had talked of two cars in every garage and a chicken in every pot. In the 1930's the chickens were in the garage and the car was going to pot. Times were beginning to be bad as 1930 closed, but the capital funds of the banking system were up from $5.9 billion to $10.3 billion and deposits had increased from $41.7 billion to $59.8 billion in the ten year period.

The decade of the 1930's brought problems that shook the foundations of many nations with a long and paralyzing depression and the beginning of the most destructive war in human history. The prophets of doom said we had reached economic maturity. Conservative men became apoplectic over $7-, $8-, and $9-billion dollar Federal budgets. The pillars of the economic firmament were falling, and an old order of things was being shaken down about our ears. Those were anxious times for anxious souls. But when we look back over the losses of those difficult years we find that although the capital funds of the banking system had declined from $10.3 billion to $8.3 billion, deposits had increased from $59.8 billion to over $71 billion in the ten years ending in 1940.

The decade from 1940 to 1950 brought the end of World War II, the greatest industrial boom in our history, and new large expenditures for defense. Deposits increased from $71 billion to $176 billion, and capital funds showed a substantial gain from $8.3 billion to $13.9 billion in only ten years. Since the end of 1950 bank deposits have increased to $211 billion and capital funds to $17.3 billion at the beginning of 1955.

As we look back over the years, it is apparent that conditions have never been normal, but the general pattern of growth of the banking system has been clear and consistent. In the last generation we have witnessed an industrial revolution as great as any in history, the development of the largest industrial plant in the world, and the most dynamic free enterprise economy banking has ever known. In every decade, in the words of John Ruskin, "There was thunder as well as dawn on the horizon." Business booms and crashes, money panics, bank runs, agricultural depressions, economic prosperity and disaster, and two major wars have occurred since the turn of the century. One might say of our free enterprise economy and the American banking system, in the words of an old, familiar verse, "The rain descended, and the floods came, and the winds blew, and beat upon that house; and it fell not; for it was founded upon a rock." Decades of hard work and dedicated services have been back of the growth of a great banking system which now serves the needs of 165 million Americans. And so we emerge from a rapid sketch of the growth of American banking.

American banks play a significant role in every segment of the nation's economic life. They are the financial intermediaries for millions of savers and for those who use the funds. They are the stewards of over $200 billion in total deposits. They determine the industrial and business channels into which a large volume of investment funds flow. By strict and wise investment decisions, banks make it imperative for businesses to operate efficiently before they can expect to have funds directed into their enterprises. This is a constructive discipline in an economy, and places upon banks social and economic responsibilities of unusual magnitude.

This review of a few of the banker's broad responsibilities is only a token indication of the significant role that the banker plays in the complex economy of his community and of the world. Imposed squarely upon him is the responsibility to manage his bank with the highest degree of proficiency. Only the most competent bank management can serve properly the banking requirements of manufacturers, distributors, retailers, farmers, consumers, savers, home owners, and local, state and national governments.

Over and above these functions in a free society where men may acquire, manage, and dispose of property, banks perform a still higher service. By discharging intelligently banking's great responsibilities, the banker plays a vital role in helping an economy of free enterprise and private property to exist and to function effectively.

In a world where men and nations are being compelled relentlessly to choose between freedom of enterprise and government control, between the rights of individual men and the encroaching powers of the state, and between private property and state ownership, the competency with which banking institutions meet their responsibilities may have far-reaching and decisive results.

If this book is helpful in providing a more widespread understanding of bank management problems and of how banking can improve its services to our people, and to our industries and business enterprises, it will have accomplished its objective.

SUGGESTED READINGS

ALLEN, FREDERICK L., *The Big Change: America Transforms Itself, 1900-1950*, New York, Harper & Brothers, 1952.

AMERICAN BANKERS ASSOCIATION, Economic Policy Commission, *Our Financial System At Work, Monetary Study No. 1*, New York, American Bankers Association, 1954.

———, *How Our Reserve System Operates, Monetary Study No. 2*, New York, American Bankers Association, 1954.

———, *Basic Issues of Monetary Policy, Monetary Study No. 6*, New York, American Bankers Association, 1954.

BOARD OF GOVERNORS OF THE FEDERAL RESERVE SYSTEM, *Annual Reports*, Washington

———, *Banking and Monetary Statistics*, Washington, 1943.

———, *Banking Studies*, Washington, The Waverly Press, 1941.

———, *Federal Reserve Bulletins*.

COUNCIL OF ECONOMIC ADVISORS, *Economic Indicators* (prepared for the Joint Committee on the Economic Report) Washington, U. S. Gov't. Printing Office (monthly).

DAVIDSON, MARSHALL BOWMAN, *Life In America;* published in association with the Metropolitan Museum of Art. Two Vols. Boston, Houghton Mifflin Company, 1951.

Economic Reports of the President, Washington, U. S. Gov't. Printing Office (annually).

HANSEN, ALVIN H., *Monetary Theory and Fiscal Policy*, New York, McGraw-Hill Book Company, Inc., 1949.

HART, A. G., *Money, Debt and Economic Activity*, New York, Prentice-Hall, Inc., 1948.

JOINT COMMITTEE ON THE ECONOMIC REPORT, *Potential Economic Growth of the United States During the Next Decade*, Washington, U. S. Gov't. Printing Office, 1954.

———, *Reports on the Economic Report of the President,* Washington, U. S. Gov't. Printing Office.

———, Subcommittee on General Credit Control and Debt Management, *Monetary Policy and the Management of the Public Debt: Their Role in Achieving Price Level Stability and High Employment,* Washington, U. S. Gov't. Printing Office, 1952.

———, *The Sustaining Economic Forces Ahead,* Washington, U. S. Gov't. Printing Office, 1952.

LYNES, RUSSELL, *The Tastemakers,* New York, Harper & Brothers, 1954.

MOULTON, H. G., *Financial Organization and the Economic System,* New York, McGraw-Hill Book Company, Inc., 1938.

SHAW, E. S., *Money, Income and Monetary Policy,* Chicago, Richard D. Irwin, Inc., 1950.

SLICHTER, SUMNER H., *The American Economy, Its Problems and Prospects,* New York, Alfred A. Knopf, Inc., 1948.

STUDENSKI, PAUL and KROOSS, HERMAN E., *Financial History of the United States,* New York, McGraw-Hill Book Company, Inc., 1952.

"U. S. A. The Permanent Revolution," *Fortune,* Vol. 43 No. 2 (February, 1951).

WILLIAMSON, HAROLD F., *The Growth of the American Economy,* New York, Prentice-Hall, Inc., 1951.

WRIGHT, CHESTER W., *Economic History of the United States,* New York, McGraw-Hill Book Company, Inc., 1949.

II

THE BANK LOAN PORTFOLIO

THE fundamental responsibility of the banking system is to supply the various types of credit demanded by producers, consumers, and investors who make up the complex pattern of our economic society.

Credit, "the currency minted of faith," around which sustained business relationships are built and around which the human attributes of confidence, courage, and ability revolve, has provided the lubricant for American industry since the founding of the Republic. The dramatic conquest of America's resources, the development of its agriculture, the construction of canals, railroads, and blast furnaces that blazed the trail for many industries—in all these credit played a significant part.

In an economy that is continuing to expand, the "intangible currency" that banks create will play a steadily increasing part in the financing of our manufacturing, commercial, transportation, and agricultural enterprises. The stream of credit will continue to broaden, to increase in complexity, and to demand greater specialized knowledge and more discriminating analysis as time goes on.

THE CREDIT FUNCTION

Specifically, what is the relationship between loans and discounts and total bank assets? How do loans and discounts affect deposit volume? How much do they contribute to bank earnings?

Table 4 shows that total loans and discounts of member

TABLE 4. LOANS AND DISCOUNTS AND TOTAL ASSETS—
FEDERAL RESERVE MEMBER BANKS

Year	Loans and Discounts (Including Overdrafts) ($ Millions)	Total Assets ($ Millions)	Loans and Discounts to Total Assets (Per Cent)
1920	19,555	32,985	59.3
1925	21,996	41,146	53.4
1930	23,870	46,395	51.4
1935	12,175	44,111	27.6
1940	15,321	62,658	24.5
1941	18,021	68,121	26.5
1942	16,088	84,917	18.9
1943	16,288	99,372	16.4
1944	18,676	118,706	15.7
1945	22,775	138,304	16.5
1946	26,696	127,241	21.0
1947	32,628	132,060	24.7
1948	36,060	131,391	27.4
1949	36,230	134,431	27.0
1950	44,705	144,660	30.9
1951	49,561	153,439	32.3
1952	55,034	160,826	34.2
1953	57,762	163,983	35.2
1954	60,250	172,242	35.0

SOURCES: *Banking and Monetary Statistics,* years 1920-40, and *Federal Reserve Bulletins,* 1941-54.

banks of the Federal Reserve System rose from $19.6 billion in 1920 to $23.9 billion in 1930.

During the mid-thirties there was a sharp drop in bank loans because of depressed economic conditions. In addition, the percentage of loans and discounts to total assets decreased sharply as increasing amounts of bank funds were invested in securities, chiefly obligations of the United States Government.

The figures for the last fifteen years show a steady upward trend in aggregate loans and discounts from $15.3 billion in 1940 to $60.2 billion in 1954, reflecting the increased economic activity which characterized this period. The percentage of loans and discounts to total assets also steadily increased during this period, except during World War II when the banking system purchased government obligations heavily to help finance military expenditures. At the same time, substantial corporate working capital accumulation, because of restricted private industrial construction, made short-term borrowing less necessary.

BANK EARNINGS

Table 5 is a summary of the sources of earnings for member banks.

It shows that the chief contributor to bank earnings since 1920 has been the income from bank loans, except during the war years when loans and discounts, as noted above, were unusually low in relation to total assets. The income from loans and discounts declined from $1.3 billion in 1930 to $498 million in 1935. Since 1935 there has been a steady increase in such income to $2.7 billion for the year 1954.

If bankers are to discharge intelligently their lending responsibilities and protect their depositors and stockholders,

TABLE 5. EARNINGS OF FEDERAL RESERVE MEMBER BANKS

Year	Income from Securities ($ Millions)	On Loans and Discounts ($ Millions)	Other Income ($ Millions)	Total Gross Income ($ Millions)	Loans and Discounts to Total Earnings (Per Cent)
1930	472	1,349	337	2,158	62
1935	467	498	242	1,207	41
1940	431	595	297	1,323	45
1945	1,136	588	378	2,102	28
1950	1,055	1,634	576	3,265	50
1953	1,263	2,632	695	4,590	57
1954	1,339	2,711	776	4,826	56

SOURCE: *Federal Reserve Bulletins.*

they must have something more than a casual acquaintance with the businesses and industries they serve. With the hazards of business life tremendous and the competitive struggle for survival and for profitable operation intense, the lending officer must have an intimate knowledge of the businesses to which he loans the bank's funds if he is to extend credit soundly.

We asked the supervisory agencies the following specific questions regarding the competency with which banks extend credit.

1. What weaknesses in lending do you find most often?

    a. Are the officers poorly qualified and trained as loaning officers?

    b. Poor credit files?

    c. Failure to get financial statements?

    d. Ignorance of the customer's business?

    e. Other weaknesses?

2. What are the most frequent causes of losses on loans?

    a. Lack of information?

    b. Poor judgment in extending credit?

    c. Other causes?

LOAN REPAYMENT PROVISIONS

One might expect that the most frequent weakness in bank lending would be the failure to require financial statements or to obtain sufficient collateral. But in the survey, twenty-eight examining agencies expressed the opinion that the most frequent weakness in bank lending, and therefore the most frequent cause of losses on loans, was the failure of the banker to require a definite repayment plan.

"The one management weakness which is most prevalent," one examining agency pointed out, "is the granting of credit with no firm understanding as to its repayment—how or when. Conversely, those bankers who require a firm understanding with borrowers as to the terms and means of repayment, maintain the soundest loan portfolios."

Commenting on the same subject, another supervisory agency wrote, "Too many loans are granted without adequate provision for periodic reduction." This together with "lax collection policies and failure to follow up when borrowers fail to meet reduction schedules are also frequent causes of losses."

ADEQUATE POLICING

A state examining supervisor described what he considers to be a common example of inadequate policing after a loan is granted. "We have had several instances," he wrote, "where retailers borrowing through the method of discounting retail installment sales contracts were permitted to make collections for the banking institution. In some cases, when the borrower failed, it was found that a substantial number of payments had been made to him but had not been remitted to the bank. In other cases, we found that the borrower had been making payments on the loan himself so that the banking institution would not know the extent of the delinquencies. It is my firm belief that banking institutions discounting consumer paper should require that payments be made direct to the institution."

The need for a repayment plan as it applies to financing consumer durable goods was emphasized by a number of the examining agencies replying to the questionnaire. One wrote that "the most frequent cause of losses on loans is the result of not having a plan of repayment and sticking to it whenever possible. In recent years banks that have gone into dealer, wholesaler, and retailer contracts without the facilities to service properly this type of financing have suffered painful losses."

"A reliance on collateral security as a deciding factor in the granting of credit," another examining agency wrote, "instead of on an analysis of the borrower's ability to repay out of earnings or conversion of earning assets, is a frequent lending weakness. In neglecting the repayment analysis," the reply continued, "the lending officer blinds himself to the hazards of collateral depreciation with resulting unrealistic appraisals. Bank management which neglects to provide for an agreement for loan repayment on terms commensurate with a borrower's ability to pay, soon loses the necessary 'leverage' over its outstanding credits. The borrowers in such instances frequently are allowed to dictate credit terms and renewals. 'Good money after bad' is a result of this loss of credit control by the banker."

Frequent mention was made of the failure to develop prompt and efficient collection measures. "Dilatory and weak collection methods are pursued, and available security is allowed to drain off. Managements have been known to prefer to make charge-offs of weakened loans rather than exert severe pressure on borrowers for liquidation."

This leniency on the part of management often is caused by existing competition from other lenders which is a wholly inadequate excuse for not enforcing a strong collection policy. This frequently results in unpremeditated loans of a capital nature which, in the aggregate, can reach a disproportionate amount of the bank's capital strength. As one examiner concluded, "In many cases our banks are partners rather than lenders."

On the other hand, a serious weakness in lending also is, "the complacent attitude toward the 'good customer of the bank.' If a borrower was an excellent risk five or ten years ago, it is assumed that he is still a good one today."

These comments suggest that it is advisable for banks

continually to re-examine their lending policies. Once a loan is made, does the banker effectively police it? Is a repayment plan agreed upon at the time the loan is made? Is there a lack of prompt and efficient collection methods? Is there sufficient detailed information that gets into the heart of the borrower's business? Is the purpose of the loan a constructive one? Is there a need for security, and does the lending officer insist upon it when the need is established? It is the unexpected developments (or failure of anticipated conditions to develop or to continue) that require a loan officer to practice constant vigilance. There must be repeated reviews of the loan commitments on the books.

BORROWER'S PERSONAL CHARACTER

One of the prime considerations in lending is the borrower's personal history and moral character. It is one of the most important factors bearing on the ability of the prospective borrower to discharge his obligation to repay.

The survey indicates, however, that in some instances possibly too much emphasis is placed on this factor at the expense of many other requirements necessary to protect the bank's position. "In those cases where there have been loan losses, it has been my observation that most of them have been due to poor processing with a tendency toward not having obtained sufficient information in the loan application and depending too much on the borrower's character.

"In connection with the more frequent causes of loan losses, it would be our considered judgment that most losses have been due to extension of credit on insufficient equities of the borrower; in other words, too much emphasis being placed on the moral side of the borrower and not sufficient attention and emphasis being directed to money-good security by the management." Another observation was, "The loan portfolios and lending policies indicate that loans too often are made on a 'good neighbor' basis rather than on sound collateral values. . . . Either the banker is hesitant about asking his borrower for a statement, or the borrower is resentful of being asked to provide one."

PYRAMIDING LOANS

Over 60 per cent of the responding agencies indicated that poor loan administration caused many loan losses. Frequently mentioned was the weakness of granting additional advances in the hope of making recovery on delinquent loans, thus allowing the borrower to abridge certain of the original covenants of his loan contract. As a consequence, the period of the loan is sometimes extended to an unreasonable length of time through the failure of the loaning officer to require the debtor to meet the terms originally contemplated when the loan contract was entered into.

One examiner found in a certain bank that "as a result of long-continued adherence to the policy of financing marginal operators and successively increasing their loans on the same collateral, the bank appears to have accumulated a heavy burden of potential sell-outs, consisting of both real estate and personal property. The collateral represented in the potential sell-outs is so voluminous in property and items of the same nature that it appears that elimination within any reasonable period would quickly absorb the limited market and further depress values which, it seems, are already declining."

"There is an inclination," another supervisory agency observed, "to allow an old customer to pyramid his borrowings with a failure on the lending agency's part to insist periodically that the borrower clear his account for a reasonable period." The expression "good money after bad" was used by two examiners. "Loans of this character which are extended constantly, but seldom regularly reduced, are defended as sound credits so long as the interest is paid. They are the so-called 'sleepers'—marginal loans which become losses and workout problems when troubles start to occur."

Often leniency can be traced to the desire to build a large loan volume without proper consideration to screening for quality and repayment ability. Specifically, "Some bankers are more concerned with collecting interest than in keeping a sound check on chattels behind the loan." "Liberal credit policies with a preference for profits rather than safety," and "Profit mindedness to increase totals often resulting in submarginal loans" are additional factors that examiners noted.

Generally, low interest rate levels cause a tendency toward lower borrowing standards which lead to an overextension of credit. In addition, it is possible that "general optimism brought about by many years of successful lending has dulled the perception of some lending officers and led to a lack of caution and wariness."

While examiners generally indicate that banks have a wide diversification of loans, it was found that "concentrations in loans are not an infrequent cause of loan weakness. Sometimes this results from too large a loan to individuals or companies, or too great an investment in a class of industry."

Another weakness was the "lack of knowledge of the financial condition of many borrowers. It is not always pleasant to pry into a customer's intimate business relationships," the report continued, "but frequently it is of vital importance to have this information." Still others, however, noted that loan losses result from a "failure . . . to take the necessary steps after adverse facts become known."

"This failure," another examining supervisor observed, "results, in some instances, in having the credit lines . . . re-written to absorb successive carry-overs from unsatisfactory operations, while in others, the obligors have been permitted to burden themselves with excessive debts by purchasing expensive machinery which has failed in sufficient productivity to enable a satisfactory reduction in loans outstanding."

BANK LOAN OFFICERS

The opinions regarding the qualifications of bank loan officers were gratifying. The replies indicated that most loaning officers were well qualified, and that poor judgment was seldom the sole cause of a loan loss. While the technical knowledge and operational experience of lending officers were considered to be adequate, an increased awareness of general economic conditions might be advisable. One interesting and comprehensive summation of this point states: "There is a failure to foresee and assess correctly local and national economic changes having an adverse bearing on credits in which the bank deals. The recent fluctuation in the . . . business is an example. A considerable over-expansion in low-quality . . . loans, both direct and indirect, has brought distress to some lenders. Other environmental factors which have caused distress, but had not been detected early enough by some bankers, developed from changing markets for cattle and some other agricultural products. Some soundly managed banks in the same communities with banks having distressed loans have not been appreciably harmed by such unfavorable economic occurrences, whereas neighboring banks less competently managed have suffered from relatively more serious problems."

Many examiners in replying to the questionnaire commented on the qualifications of bank officers. The following are a few sample excerpts:

"It is rare to find officers poorly qualified and trained as loan officials."

"With few exceptions officers are well or reasonably well qualified."

"Credit officers appear to be adequately qualified and trained as loaning officers."

"For the most part our loaning officers are reasonably well trained and qualified."

AIDS TO MANAGEMENT

During the past twenty years there has been an enormous increase in the business tools available to help bankers evaluate the lending problems that cross their desks every day. The reliable and refined economic and monetary data published by the Federal Reserve Banks, Departments of Commerce, Agriculture, and Labor, Joint Committee on the Economic Report, the research projects of business schools and trade associations, and the vast store of knowledge in business and technical journals are invaluable sources of information that bankers should study and analyze more vigorously than they have in the past.

SUMMARY

With 35 per cent of bank assets invested in loans and discounts, and with over half of gross earnings the result of loaning activities, the comments on this phase of bank management are significant. Adding further emphasis to this view was the fact that 57 per cent of the forty-six replies advanced similar answers to the query on the cause of loan losses. It was their collective opinion that the absence of a closely administered loan repayment plan was the most frequent cause of losses on loans. Failure to outline and to agree upon a definite loan repayment plan at the time the loan is made is a serious error. To neglect to see that a repayment plan is followed is to invite losses. A loan is only proved good when it is paid.

Another weakness in lending was the tendency to emphasize the borrower's collateral as security for repayment instead of stressing his ability to repay out of earnings. Also noted frequently were such weaknesses as inefficient collection procedures, risk renewals or pyramiding of doubtful loans, and subordinating sound loan standards to increased interest income.

The lending of money is a traditional function of the banking business. The judgments, the decisions, and the policies that bankers make in their loan operations determine not only the progress of their banks, but also in a large measure the growth and economic welfare of the nation. Bank credit is the lifeline of the country's economic activity, and the loan making function of commercial banks constitutes one of the significant phases of bank administration. Bankers must constantly examine the everyday fundamentals of sound loan administration if they are to extend credit soundly and so meet properly the legitimate credit needs of their respective communities.

SUGGESTED READINGS

AMERICAN BANKERS ASSOCIATION, Bank Management Commission, *Commercial Bank Investment Policy*, Publication No. *126*, New York, American Bankers Association, 1951.

———, Economic Policy Commission, *Loans, Investments and Interest Rates, Monetary Study No. 3*, New York, American Bankers Association, 1954.

———, *Manual of Laws Relating to Loans and Investments by National Banks*, New York, American Bankers Association, 1949.

BOGEN, JULES I., ed., *Financial Handbook*, New York, The Ronald Press, 1948.

CHANDLER, LESTER V., *The Economics of Money and Banking*, New York, Harper & Brothers, 1953.

FOULKE, ROY A., *Practical Financial Statement Analysis*, New York, McGraw-Hill Book Company, Inc., 1953.

PRATHER, C. L., *Money and Banking*, Chicago, Richard D. Irwin, Inc., 1953.

ROBINSON, ROLAND I., *The Management of Bank Funds*, New York, McGraw-Hill Book Company, Inc., 1951.

WESTERFIELD, RAY B., *Money, Credit and Banking*, New York, The Ronald Press, 1947.

III

THE CREDIT FILES OF THE BANK

INFORMATION is one key to successful loan administration.

Without the exact facts which the credit file should contain, no banker can reach a sound credit decision. Inadequate and insufficient business records about the borrower and his company are inexcusable. The responsibility to maintain a written record—the credit file—is so important that it cannot be casually dismissed because office personnel and time are limited.

Antecedent information about the borrower, balance sheets, financial statements, surplus accounts, budgets and other auxiliary records, coupled with the ability to analyze and interpret the information intelligently after it is obtained are fundamental responsibilities that cannot be avoided. Credit judgment needs to be based on the experienced interpretation of essential facts. There is no place for guess work in making loans when facts are obtainable. Credit files must be complete and must be kept up to date constantly if snap judgments and excessive loan losses are to be avoided.

Economic and business conditions change rapidly, and they will continue to change because change is inherent in our economic system. The banker must be constantly aware of the importance of having the customer furnish financial information regularly, so that he can keep continuously abreast of the debtor's financial condition and the effect that changing business conditions may have upon his business. If the banker has at his disposal complete credit information gathered from all available sources, he can approach his lending problem with an intelligent understanding of the borrower's request for money. Full knowledge of the debtor's business is also necessary to make an intelligent analysis of the credit risk. These are essential if a sound well thought out loan decision is to be made.

BUSINESS FAILURES

One index of changing business and economic conditions is business failures. The decade following the end of World War II was characterized generally by exceptionally active business with production, employment, and profits at high levels. Notwithstanding this, but reflecting the dynamics of a free enterprise and competitive economy, business failures have been increasing each year with the exception of the early fifties, when Korean hostilities greatly stimulated business activity. The average number of failures for this period, however, was about one-third the average of the years 1924-38.

As shown in Table 6, during 1946, the first postwar year, there were 1129 business failures. During 1948, 5250 business enterprises were forced into bankruptcy, and in 1949, reflecting the mild recession of that year, business failures almost doubled.

Following the Korean settlement, business began to return

to prewar conditions of formidable but healthy and stimulating competition. Business failures also began to increase. In 1954, they were up 25 per cent over the previous year and reached a postwar high of 11,086.

TABLE 6. BUSINESS POPULATION AND BUSINESS FAILURES
(*Selected Years*)

Year	Number of Businesses	Number of Failures
1929	3,029,000	22,909
1932	2,828,100	31,822
1935	2,991,900	12,244
1940	3,290,800	13,619
1945	3,113,900	809
1946	3,487,200	1,129
1947	3,783,200	3,474
1948	3,948,300	5,250
1949	4,000,000	9,246
1950	4,050,700	9,162
1951	4,108,500	8,058
1952	4,167,400	7,611
1953	4,193,900	8,862
1954	Not Yet Available	11,086

SOURCE: U. S. Government, *Economic Report of the President*, January 1955.

LOAN LOSSES

Table 7 reflects the importance of adequate credit information by showing loan losses for the period 1930-54.

Total losses on loans during the 25-year period 1930-54 reached the staggering total of $4486 million. The percentage of loan charge-offs to capital was highest during the depression of the early thirties. Losses declined as business activity

TABLE 7. LOSSES OF FEDERAL RESERVE MEMBER BANKS ON LOANS
AND DISCOUNTS—1930-54

Year	Amount of Loans and Discounts (*$ Millions*)	Total Charge-offs on Loans and Discounts (*$ Millions*)	Total Capital (*$ Millions*)	Charge-offs to Total Capital (*Per Cent*)
1930	23,870	195	6,593	3.0
1931	19,261	295	5,999	4.9
1932	15,204	403	5,409	7.4
1933	12,833	425	4,962	8.6
1934	12,028	452	5,054	8.9
1935	12,175	252	5,145	4.9
1936	13,360	207	5,275	3.9
1937	13,958	105	5,371	2.0
1938	13,208	122	5,424	2.2
1939	13,962	108	5,522	2.0
1940	15,321	90	5,698	1.6
1941	18,021	84	5,886	1.4
1942	16,088	65	6,101	1.1
1943	16,288	63	6,475	1.0
1944	18,676	60	6,968	0.9
1945	22,775	47	7,589	0.6
1946	26,696	61	8,095	0.8
1947	32,628	103	8,464	1.2
1948	36,060	271	8,801	3.1
1949	36,230	210	9,174	2.3
1950	44,705	180	9,695	1.8
1951	49,561	193	10,218	1.9
1952	55,034	149	10,761	1.4
1953	57,762	132	11,316	1.2
1954	60,250	214	12,210	1.8

Total Loan Losses 1930-54—$4486 million

SOURCE: Board of Governors, *Banking and Monetary Statistics*, 1930-41, and
Call Reports of Member Banks for 1942-54. Charge-offs on Loans and
Discounts 1942-54 from *Federal Reserve Bulletins*.

increased from 1935 to 1937, but increased again when another recession started in the fall of 1937 and continued until 1939 when war preparations began in earnest.

Beginning in 1940, there was a steady decline in loan losses during the prosperous war and early postwar years, but the downward trend was again reversed by a recession that occurred in 1948-49. During the Korean War, when business was active, losses on loans declined, and they continued at a low rate through 1954.

The record shows conclusively the need for protection against periods of sharp recession in business. A bank's capital and surplus is the first line of defense for the protection of depositors. Loose loan administration inevitably will lead to excessive charges to the capital accounts that endanger the bank's solvency.

There is little doubt that inefficient credit analysis and investigation has been one of the fundamental causes over the years of most bank failures. The failure to gather and store adequate credit information in complete files is irresponsible and inexcusable.

THE NEED FOR CREDIT FILES

The examiners indicated that there is an increasing need for adequate credit files and careful analysis and evaluation of credit information by bank loaning officers.

Even though bankers are becoming "credit file minded," over half of those replying to the questionnaire suggested that the credit files of some banks either were poor or were not kept current with interim profit and loss figures and balance sheets.

INCOMPLETE FILES

To quote one typical report, "In some instances, credit files do not contain adequate written information regarding the borrower and his business, although the bankers claim to know all essential particulars. With small exceptions, balance sheets are not audited and some of them are found to be over a year old. Current profit and loss statements are missing in many cases, and without an income statement, the balance sheets tell only part of the story. Pro forma statements are seldom found in credit files. Comparative figures showing the trend of the business are completely missing."

On the other hand, one agency "doubted if there were many instances where the importance of credit files is now minimized. Considerable progress in the past twenty years has been made in this particular phase of loaning policies." "However," the report continued, "the credit files are not as complete as they should be." This same examining agency observed "that the interim statements, especially on borrowers whose loans carry unusual risk, are not always obtained. Operating data and operating statements on sizable credits are always required by the bank, whereas such information should be on hand for all credits. Audited statements rather than statements prepared by the borrowing entity are not stressed often enough."

CONFERENCES WITH BORROWERS

"Loaning officers frequently fail to 'talk' to the credit files through memoranda on important conferences with the borrower. Visits to the borrower's plant or place of business often are not noted in the file. . . . Such memoranda," the agency added, "are especially important if in the course of such visits information is obtained which indicates a possible change in the borrower's industry or in the relative position of the borrower within the industry." The report also stressed the value of noting in the file "the loaning officer's own individual feeling toward the management of the borrower and his opinion of the firm's progress or lack of progress."

FAILURE TO MAINTAIN CURRENT FILES

Often mentioned was the failure of bankers to keep their credit files up to date. The failure to replace old statements with current ones was a frequent criticism. Perhaps even more significant, as one supervisory agency noted, is the "failure to compare a new statement when it is received with an old statement in order to determine the firm's progress or retrogression." One examining agency noted that while "most credit files are in reasonably good shape, banker's have a definite tendency to keep outdated papers and insurance policies in current files." In a similar vein, one reply noted that "most small banks do not carry on a continuing build up of their credit files."

It is essential that an active credit file be maintained complete with current information necessary for an intelligent and immediate consideration of the credit problem. It not only is embarrassing to the lending officer, but it is irritating to the customer if his application for a loan is delayed because the credit department has failed to compile an adequate credit file. Inadequate knowledge of a borrower's financial condition can lead to substantial lending losses. When the credit files are up to date, the banker can more easily carry out his responsibility to loan wisely for the protection of the borrower, the bank, and the community.

OBTAINING ADEQUATE CREDIT INFORMATION

The failure to ask the borrower for the information necessary for a complete credit file was mentioned several times. One agency commenting in some detail wrote, "Many banks do not obtain adequate credit information. Statements are not obtained from borrowers, or those on file carry stale dates. Other essential credit information is not procured. No analysis is made in written form of statements and other credit information. . . . In other instances," the comment continued, "statements often are incomplete, undated, unsigned, or in error. In short, credit files in many banks are incomplete and not well organized. Not an infrequent cause of problem loans is the failure to be accurately informed about the business of credit applicants. This may occur in two ways, that is, ignorance of the kind of business, or insufficient information about a particular business. This in turn may lead to commitments of a speculative type, especially in the case of new and untried ventures."

Another reply summarized this condition by saying, "Our examiners frequently report difficulty in having banks obtain current financial statements. Either the banker is hesitant about asking his borrower for a statement, or the borrower is resentful of being asked to provide one."

Since every business concern periodically must prepare a statement of condition, a banker is not imposing upon his customer when he requests a copy. To loan money to a business manager who does not draw up balance sheet and profit and loss statements for his business at regular intervals is not sound banking. Complete statements of a business will often answer critical questions. No management that has asked for a bank loan should object to furnishing the lending officer with all the information necessary for him to ascertain the borrower's financial status. The more the banker knows about the borrower, the more he can tactfully help the borrower avoid unsound financial policies and practices.

RELYING ON PERSONAL KNOWLEDGE

Mention frequently was made of the tendency for lending officers in smaller banks to keep credit information "in their heads" instead of in a credit file. One examiner commented, "There is frequently much to be desired as far as credit files are concerned. This is especially true when the bank is small and the loaning officer through long tenure carries a great fund of credit knowledge in his head."

Another noted that "in the rural districts, bank officers are personally acquainted with borrowers and rely on personal knowledge." On the other hand, one examiner said, "While the failure to maintain complete credit files is a weakness, especially in the smaller institutions, this is perhaps offset to some extent by closer personal knowledge of the borrower, but too often this is kept in the lender's mind. There is a frequent lack of proper historical memoranda." Or, as one state examining official put it, "Bank officers in rural areas rely too heavily on personal knowledge and acquaintance, and not enough on credit information."

Significant facts regarding the establishment, development, and business success of a prospective borrower are imperative. It is no easy assignment to run a business successfully. Of the entire 4 million business concerns in existence, the

Department of Commerce estimated in 1951 that only 45 per cent, less than half, were five years or more of age. There must be a modern, well organized credit department as the focal point for all the facts the bank collects about the customer. Such a credit department makes possible a continuing and permanent record of a borrower's background. If such a record exists only in the memory of one of the officers of the bank, all the credit information goes with the officer when he leaves.

SOURCES OF CREDIT INFORMATION

The complexities of lending operations today call for credit files which include financial statements, investigations, letters, institutional reports, and other financial and personal details of the borrower. There are many sources of information about the borrower. Reports from other banks and other businesses in the same trade, investment manuals, newspapers, periodicals and directories, public records, and the mercantile agencies are just a few of the sources of information available to the credit department. Indispensable, of course, are the borrower's statements prepared by independent accountants. When this is not possible, some of the larger banks follow the alternative of having their own accounting staffs examine the borrower's books and records and of preparing the appropriate statements.

PERSONAL INTERVIEWS

Not to be overlooked is the value of personal interviews with the customer. Nothing can substitute for a visit to the borrower's place of business. This permits the banker to see first hand the borrower's plant, equipment, operations, and labor relations in action. Though vital and necessary information can be obtained from other sources, the knowledge that is gained from the personal interview is one of the most valuable sources of credit information. Comments concerning this point are interesting. A typical, critical response was, "There is no indication of checkups on a borrower's business through visits or otherwise."

The assets and liabilities of a company, the surplus statement, the profit and loss statements, and other statistical measures merely reflect the policies and decisions of the management staff. Personal interviews go behind the figures and provide comprehensive and factual information that cannot be obtained any other way.

VERIFYING CREDIT INFORMATION

Sometimes it is necessary to verify an inventory valuation independently of the accounting records. In one business where a satisfactory relationship seemed to exist between the current assets and the current liabilities, the banker noted that borrowings had been steady for three years. An examination showed that the inventory, particularly work-in-process, constituted a large part of the total assets. The auditor who had prepared the balance sheet had stated in the typical manner that the inventory had been certified by a responsible member of the management staff. The loaning officer had at first accepted this assertion, but subsequent study revealed that the inventory was actually 45 per cent overvalued. Some items were ten to fifteen years old and absolutely worthless. Thousands of dollars worth of merchandise could not even be located. Some goods had been out on consignment as long as five years, and in all but one case the concerns to which the goods had been consigned were either bankrupt or out of business.

As a substantial portion of the bank's loan portfolio consists of working capital loans, an accurate inventory valuation is important. We need always to remember that during any period of inflation, marginal and poorly managed businesses often exist because they make money on the rising value of commodities and inventories. The real test of management comes during a period of price decline. Historically, when commodity and inventory values decline sharply, the marginal manager and his business have financial trouble.

FAILURE TO ACT ON INFORMATION AVAILABLE

Although many different deficiencies in bank credit files were described by over half of the replies, none listed any one as a major cause of loan losses. Instead, some replies indicated that the failure to act on the information available is a "frequent cause of losses on loans." One examiner noted that his experiences showed, "While financial and operating statements are usually secured, frequently they are not carefully analyzed, but are merely placed in the credit files." Another examiner expressed it this way: "Rather than ignorance of the customer's business, I would say that a greater weakness is the failure or inability to analyze the borrower's financial statements and operating statements and the failure to evaluate properly the information that is available."

In other words, not only is there a failure to obtain current information, up-to-date statements, and interim operating figures, but perhaps even more important, according to the forty-six agencies answering the questionnaire, is the failure to analyze carefully and to evaluate accurately the material that is in the credit files. As one agency put it, "Too often the information in the credit files appears to have been assembled only to the extent necessary to satisfy statutory and supervisory requirements with little use apparently being made of it in granting or servicing of the loan. This is evident by the fact that examiners' reports noted credit weaknesses, *apparent from the files,* but not acted upon by the management.

"The quality of credit files is usually in direct proportion to management's understanding of their value," the same report continued. "Surprisingly enough, there are few banks which do not make some effort to obtain financial statements —at least a signed statement form with a date they hope will satisfy the examiners. However, such statements are frequently meaningless where the banker has not required a reconciliation of net worth between periods by the furnishing of operating statements." Here again, the advantageous interpretation of credit information is neglected, even in those cases where worthwhile data might be available from furnished statements. "There are few bankers," an examiner wrote, "who do not have some knowledge of each customer's business. However, it is the current applicability of such knowledge which varies with the banker. This knowledge is generally dependent upon a requirement of current credit information from the borrower."

LEGAL DOCUMENTS

While a banker must assume risks in the extension of credit, it is significant that several examiners pointed out weaknesses in the establishment of the legal aspects of a loan. A surprising number of losses result from the bank having no claim against the borrower because of inadequate legal provisions, overlooking necessary legal forms, or failure to consult with legal counsel in unusual loan cases. One reply stated that "there is a lack of knowledge of banking law, negotiable instruments, liens, uniform trust receipts, marshaling of liens, and other important restrictive legislation. This is a very definite weakness among bankers."

Another comment was, "Lack of appraisals, insurance, title opinions, collateral assignment, borrowing authorization, and credit information are all common weaknesses."

The following comment was made by a national examining agency in its critical analysis of the operation of a bank: "The credit files contain few current property statements, and although numerous credit lines are dependent upon earnings for liquidation, no operating statements are held. Real estate and chattel mortgage lines are accepted and carried without appraisal, inspection, or checking the pledged collateral, and in many instances the lien instruments are carried unrecorded. No title information is required on the collateral, and apparently no activity is conducted to determine that good title is held, or that the property is free of encumbrance. The management requires no insurance on pledged automobiles, and numerous exceptions exist with reference to insurance on real estate improvements.

"Furthermore, the meager credit information that is available appears to have been obtained largely at the behest of examiners and, apparently, merely for their use, for it is inconceivable that the condition of the institution would have been permitted to develop if the management had been fully aware of the existing circumstances. Reference to previous reports of examination will reveal that lack of knowledge of the actual conditions surrounding the various lines has been a long standing cause of criticism but without results."

An additional comment concerning legal matters was, "The failure 'to tie up' security so that there is no chance of it being taken away from the bank in case of bankruptcy, fraud, misappropriation, or by other creditors is one of the principal troubles we find in banks." According to another supervisory agency, "When security is obtained, it is not tied down tight enough, with correct description and serial numbers on trust receipts or enough itemization and description in chattel mortgages."

"False information sometimes given by the borrower—the failure to check thoroughly all submitted information and failure to check into and follow up the personal life of the borrower for unwarranted spending and luxurious living habits is an important matter," wrote a state examiner. He mentioned a recent failure of a large real estate developer where "personal habits should have acted as a 'red flag' but were ignored, i.e., profligate spending, the most expensive cars, yachts, and town and summer homes."

"The importance of vigilant policing of the collateral, such as accounts receivable, notes or conditional sales contracts receivable, inventory, chattel, or any other similar capital assets of a borrower when pledged to secure his obligations cannot be overemphasized," one examiner wrote. "Unless a bank has both the intent and facilities adequately to police these types of security, it can invite losses, as this office has often observed."

As much caution should be practiced in the legal details of a bank loan as is practiced in gathering analytical information. With the growth of commercial banking, there have been an increasing number of court decisions concerning banking transactions. This makes imperative the need for legal provisions that cover any contingencies that may arise in connection with a loan. The bank should without fail obtain all the necessary legal papers that are applicable to the particular credit problem. In the more complicated loans, legal counsel should be obtained.

CREDIT FILE QUESTIONS

Several organizations can be helpful to banks when a credit file problem arises. Robert Morris Associates have made significant contributions to the field of bank credit policies and practices. The American Bankers Association, the state bankers' associations, and the Federal Reserve Banks have developed valuable information on credit and related subjects which is available in texts, pamphlets, and a variety of technical manuals. There are available also the services of your correspondent bank, which services include assistance in the solution of credit file problems.

SUMMARY

Half of the replies indicated that credit files of banks under their jurisdictions were not complete and up to date. Among the deficiencies reported were a lack of audited statements, an absence of interim financial information about the borrower, and the loaning officer's own appraisal of the current status of the account.

Often stressed was the tendency of lending officers to keep pertinent credit information "in their heads," particularly historical information that belonged in the files so the bank could have a complete and permanent financial record of its borrowing customers.

There was frequent mention of loan losses occurring as a result of the failure of bankers to act promptly upon the information that was available, indicating that loaning officers may not evaluate properly all the facts that are in the credit files.

Bankers have in recent years enjoyed unusually low loss ratios because of unprecedented business conditions. Should business return to lower volume and smaller profits, marginal businesses will have trouble and losses will occur. Bankers can minimize these losses by gathering the essential credit information upon which to base loan decisions.

SUGGESTED READINGS

CHAPIN, ALBERT F., *Credit and Collection Principles and Practices,* New York, McGraw-Hill Book Company, Inc., 1953.

COMAN, EDWIN T., *Sources of Business Information,* New York, Prentice-Hall, Inc., 1949.

ETTINGER, RICHARD P. and GOLIEB, DAVID E., *Credits and Collections,* New York, Prentice-Hall, Inc., 1949.

PROCHNOW, HERBERT V. and FOULKE, ROY A., *Practical Bank Credit,* New York, Prentice-Hall, Inc., 1950.

WILLIAMS, CHARLES W., ed., *The Credit Department, A Training Ground for the Bank Loan Officer,* Philadelphia, Robert Morris Associates, 1954.

IV

THE BANK BOND PORTFOLIO

INVESTMENTS in the obligations of the United States Government are one of the major earning assets of the commercial banks in the United States. This is a recent development paralleling the growth in the debt of the Federal government. The bond accounts of the banks grew in relative importance during the middle thirties with the deficit financing undertaken for public works, followed by much larger expenditures and deficits as our defense outlays mounted.

The banks' government bond accounts assumed an even more significant role during World War II when vastly greater sums were expended by the United States for military purposes. It was the intention of the monetary authorities that the bonds issued to finance the war deficit be purchased and held by non-bank investors, and as a consequence the banks were not permitted to subscribe to issues floated in the last six war loan drives. However, because of the maintenance of "the pattern of rates" decided upon early in the war and because of the magnitude of the war deficits, the close of World War II found the commercial banks of the country holding nearly 60 per cent of the national debt.[1]

---

[1] For a more complete exposition, see Karl R. Bopp, "Three Decades of Federal Reserve Policy" in *Post War Economic Studies, No. 8,* November 1947, published by the Board of Governors of the Federal Reserve System.

UNITED STATES GOVERNMENT BONDS

More specifically, the amount of U. S. Government obligations held by the member banks of the Federal Reserve System, as well as the percentage of total assets so invested, has
increased substantially in the last decade and a half. In 1928,
for example, as shown in Table 8, the member banks of the

TABLE 8. TOTAL ASSETS AND INVESTMENTS IN U. S. GOVERNMENT
BONDS—FEDERAL RESERVE MEMBER BANKS
(Selected Years)

Year	Total Assets (*$ Millions*)	Investment in U.S. Government Bonds	
		(*$ Millions*)	Per Cent of Total Assets
1928	48,258	4,312	8.9
1935	44,111	12,268	27.8
1940	62,658	15,823	25.2
1945	138,304	78,338	56.6
1950	144,660	52,365	36.2
1951	153,439	51,621	33.6
1952	160,826	52,763	32.8
1953	168,983	52,603	31.1
1954	172,242	57,809	33.6

SOURCE: Board of Governors, *Banking and Monetary Statistics,* 1928-40, and
Federal Reserve Bulletins for 1945-54.

United States had $4312 million or 8.9 per cent of their assets
invested in obligations of the Federal government. In seven
short years, by 1935, the dollar value of U. S. Government
obligations held by the member banks had almost tripled,
and totaled $12,268 million, accounting for about 28 per
cent of their assets. During the next decade, because of the
large sums expended for military defense and war purposes,
the holdings of government securities by the member banks

increased six-fold and on December 31, 1945, exceeded $78 billion. Of the total assets of member banks, over 56 per cent was invested in U. S. Government securities.

POSTWAR LOAN EXPANSION

In the postwar period production facilities were expanded and industrial production soared as the pent-up worldwide demand was made effective. Despite the production achievements of American industry, demand greatly exceeded supply and prices rose. As a consequence, banks were called upon to expand their loans for a number of important reasons. First, since one of the best ways to halt an inflation is to increase the supply of goods available, banks increased their loans as business demanded more and more bank credit in order to expand productive facilities and increase output. This expansion of bank credit changed the relative composition of bank assets. The volume of investments in government bonds decreased while loans rose. Member bank holdings of United States Government securities decreased about 33 per cent between 1945 and 1950, from over $78 billion to $52 billion. In addition, total assets of all member banks increased during the same period, reflecting the increase in bank loans. As a consequence, the percentage of the total assets of the member banks invested in U. S. Government obligations declined from 56 per cent in 1945 to 36 per cent five years later.

THE KOREAN OUTBREAK

Following the outbreak of hostilities in Korea in 1950, military expenditures were substantially increased, again calling for an increase in bank credit and a growth in the money supply. During this period, as the national debt increased, bank holdings of United States Government obligations held constant, although representing a slightly declining percentage of total assets. As of December 31, 1954, holdings of government securities accounted for 34 per cent of the total assets of member banks.

INCOME FROM GOVERNMENT SECURITIES

Another way of measuring the significance of the bond portfolio of the commercial banks is to consider the percentage of gross earnings accounted for by interest income on government securities.

In the period prior to World War II, published data do not separate interest on government obligations from income received on other securities.

In more recent years, interest received by member banks on United States Government securities as reported in Table 9 shows that such income, in 1945, accounted for about 47 per cent of gross income. As bank loans increased in the postwar years, and interest rates were permitted to rise after the Federal Reserve-Treasury accord in March 1951, interest income from United States Government bond investments as a percentage of gross earnings declined about 50 per cent. In 1954, for example, income from this source accounted for about 22 per cent of total earnings.

In view of the significance of United States Government obligations in the total assets of banks, one of the major parts of the questionnaire was devoted to the bond portfolio. The first question asked was:

"What weaknesses in handling the bond account do you

find most often?" and included thereunder two related points, namely, "poor spacing of maturities" and "reaching for yields."

TABLE 9. TOTAL GROSS EARNINGS AND INTEREST INCOME ON U. S. GOVERNMENT SECURITIES—FEDERAL RESERVE MEMBER BANKS

(*Selected Years*)

		Interest on U.S. Govt. Securities	
Year	Gross Earnings (*$ Millions*)	(*$ Millions*)	Per Cent of Total Earnings
1928	2,194	498	22.7[a]
1935	1,207	467	38.7[a]
1940	1,323	431	32.6[a]
1945	2,102	997	47.4
1950	3,265	865	26.5
1951	3,669	832	22.7
1952	4,120	929	22.5
1953	4,590	1,011	22.0
1954	4,826	1,066	22.1

SOURCE: Board of Governors, *Banking and Monetary Statistics,* 1928-40, and *Federal Reserve Bulletins* for 1945-54.
[a] Includes interest on other securities.

REPLIES TO THE QUESTIONNAIRE

The replies indicate that in general the bond portfolios of the banks of the United States are reasonably well managed. The large metropolitan banks have specially trained skilled staffs managing their portfolios. As a consequence, their bonds are generally well handled. However, many banks, especially those with a small number of officers, have a real and practical problem of bond portfolio management.

First, there is the over-all problem of acquiring the fundamental knowledge and skill required for sound investment management; and *second,* there is the practical limitation of time. In a small bank, the staff is obliged to devote most of its time to directing the operations of the bank in relation to the banking needs of the local community. Many of these smaller banks properly rely to a considerable degree on their city correspondents for advice and counsel. Many of these banks also seek the advice of investment banking concerns.

BANKS REACH FOR YIELDS

Notwithstanding this policy, however, nearly half the agencies said that there is a tendency to "reach for yields," with, of course, the consequent sacrifice of safety, as well as some poor spacing of maturities. This is a result in part of the lack of basic knowledge of the whole subject of bond investments.

One supervisor put it this way: "Because the small or medium-sized institution operates under a handicap in managing its bond portfolio, there is a tendency for certain weaknesses to develop. The individual who makes the investment decisions lacks the time to study his problems thoroughly, and he is also likely to be ill-equipped for the work. Thus, it is not surprising to find that securities are sold to the bank on the basis of high yield instead of their superior quality. The poorly informed bank official may not be able to discriminate carefully between qualitative characteristics of different issues of securities. He will accept the issue which is represented to him as being of suitable quality and pick the one with the most attractive rate of return. The result of such a policy applied over a period of time will be unfortunate to the portfolio quality-wise."

THE MATURITY PROBLEM

The same bank examining agency, emphasizing the maturity aspect of the problem, continued: "At best, the arrangement of maturities in a bond portfolio is not an easy task. For the part-time investment officer who is typically charged with responsibility for managing the bond portfolio in a small or medium-sized bank, maturity selection often is ignored. In part, this may be explained by the lack of time to find the appropriate selection of maturities for bond issues. Also, it is possible that the bank officer merely overlooks the importance of arranging his maturities in such a manner that an appropriate volume of funds will flow from the investment account with a minimum of reliance upon markets. Finally, there is also the possibility that the uninitiated in the investment field will not appreciate the grave risks that stem from too great reliance upon the market place when it is necessary to convert the bond account into cash."

Another supervisor stated that reaching for yields "is a fault of 50 per cent of smaller banks." Another described the poor spacing of maturities as "the most frequent weakness we find in the bond accounts of our banks."

DEPOSIT FLUCTUATIONS

A bank's pattern of deposit fluctuations also should be considered in the management of a bond portfolio, especially in planning the maturity schedule. There is a suggestion in the replies that banks should anticipate their seasonal requirements. One bank examining supervisor worded it this way: "A sufficient volume of appropriate short-term securities is not maintained in some instances to provide liquidity for deposit fluctuations, seasonal changes, semi-permanent withdrawals, and funds for loans. This is sometimes revealed in the unbalanced ratio of government and other bonds to the total bond account, with liquidity in some cases being largely dependent on short and intermediate term municipals of a not-too-readily marketable type." The supervisor went on to suggest that bankers should carefully study and systematically review "deposit fluctuations and the seasonal need for funds or loans, and adjust the short maturities in the government bond account accordingly."

PROBLEMS OF MANAGEMENT

A bank with limited official personnel finds it difficult to assign one or more officers and a fixed part of their time to the responsibility of managing the bond portfolio. However, this responsibility is so important, accounting as it does for approximately one-third of the assets of the banks of the United States, and about 20 per cent of their gross earnings, that it cannot be casually dismissed because official personnel and time are limited.

One of the questions included in this Survey of bank management considered this point. The examining agencies were asked if the responsibility for the bond account of banks was centralized in any one person. Of the agencies replying to the survey, only 40 per cent said that this important responsibility was centralized and definitely assigned as it should be. In other words, an analysis of the replies suggests that about six out of ten found this lack of centralized responsibility to be a frequent weakness in the management of the bond accounts of the banks.

"The absence of a clearly stated and generally understood investment policy," another agency wrote, "the application of which is definitely assigned to a single individual, is one of the important weaknesses in bond account management for the small or medium-sized bank. Sometimes the management group does not appreciate the importance of reducing its investment policy to a clean-cut statement. Then again it may lack the necessary skills for preparing this statement because local community problems dominate its interest. Even if there is an investment policy program for the bank, the difficulties inherent in a shortage of managerial personnel greatly complicate the task of applying the policy to the bond account."

OVER-TRADING THE BOND ACCOUNT

Included in one reply was a case history of a bank with total resources of $2,600,000 and capital accounts of $146,-000 illustrating the pitfalls of excessive bond trading for speculative profit. While acknowledging that this case is an extreme one, the agency pointed out that it demonstrates how a poorly managed, speculative investment program can impair a bank's soundness despite the "investment" in generally acceptable quality issues. These trading activities were pursued by the management despite the contrary recommendations of the supervisory examiners.

A study of the three most recent examination reports of

the bank revealed that the institution had been trading in securities on an almost unbelievable scale. Each successive examination report shows a substantial growth in the number and size of transactions accompanying a sharp decline in their average profitability. Table 10 summarizes pertinent data regarding the trading activities of this bank.

TABLE 10

	(Period A) One Year Ago January 24 to April 16	(Period B) Two Years Ago April 19 to January 24	(Period C) Three Years Ago March 28 to April 19
Bonds purchased	$2,652,170	$1,050,059	$808,758
Bonds sold	$2,429,335	$1,054,919	$729,895
Balance of security portfolio end of period	$ 715,985	$ 493,150	$498,010
Number issues sold	84	56	62
Number issues purchased	84	46	56
Profits on securities sold	$ 11,339	$ 8,113	$ 9,536
Average profit per $1000 bond	$ 4.67	$ 7.69	$ 13.06
Sales to total assets	111 per cent	71 per cent	50 per cent
Sales to total securities	339 per cent	214 per cent	150 per cent
Sales to total capital	1959 per cent	996 per cent	702 per cent

"As shown by Table 10, bond sales during Period A, the most recent, totaled about $2.5 million, and were four times as large as they were three years earlier during Period C. Sales during Period C equaled ½ of the bank's total assets; 1½ times its security account, and 7 times its capital. Three years later, covered by Period A, the volume of sales had increased to such an extent that they exceeded the bank's total assets; were equal to 3⅓ times its security account and nearly 20 times its capital account.

"About one year after Period A, the accumulated book profit from security trading was approximately $40,000. Due to the considerable supervisory apprehension over this situation, this latest examination included an extensive analysis of the entire account. Between examinations the total turnover had amounted to $10 million in a portfolio grown to approximately $1.9 million book value on the date of examination. All bonds were municipal issues with low coupons and long maturities. Over 80 per cent matured after twenty years with the remainder due in ten to twenty years."

The inevitable consequence of this policy is described in a short memorandum in the Examiner's files.

"As a result of continued excessive trading in municipal securities, principally low coupon, long maturities, through a dealer with an unsavory reputation, and the sharp decline in price in issues of this class, there existed a depreciation in the security account of $270,000 on the date of examination, which rendered the bank wholly insolvent. Past losses were not taken on issues sold but concealed by a write-up of issues bought, made possible by fictitious billings by the dealer.

"The rehabilitation of this bank required a contribution of $200,000 by the directors to absorb the losses which were entailed in the orderly correction of this untenable investment position."

INADEQUATE KNOWLEDGE OF BONDS

Other supervisory agencies were of the opinion that the lack of knowledge of bond portfolio management was the cause of the weaknesses they found in bond accounts. More specifically, about 57 per cent of the replies received cited this as a weakness although about half of them added that it was true only in a few instances.

One state supervisory agency reported, "The weakness in handling the bond account that we find most often is the lack of adequate knowledge on the whole subject of bonds. We must state that we are talking about a few small banks. The large state banks which hold most of the assets of the state banking system are undoubtedly among the best equipped banks in the world to analyze bond accounts, to space maturities properly, and to buy the proper kind of bonds. They do not stretch out for yields and the responsibility is centralized for handling the account.

"Most of the small banks in the state do fairly well, because most of them depend on correspondent banks to handle the bond account for them. A few cases, and they are very few in relation to the total, will show weakness merely because there is a lack of an adequate knowledge of the whole subject of bonds.

"Generally speaking we would say that we have little trouble, very small as far as the total in dollars and cents go, and very little trouble, comparatively speaking, as to the bond account."

SUMMARY

The replies disclosed that bank bond portfolios generally are well managed. The large metropolitan banks have specially trained staffs who manage their bond accounts competently. However, in some banks the staff is obliged to devote most of its time to directing other operations of the bank and attending to the banking needs of the community. As a consequence, the responsibility of managing the bond portfolio is not specifically assigned. Sixty per cent noted this weakness.

Occasionally, bond investment policy is not clearly defined or the seasonal liquidity needs of the bank are not sufficiently analyzed. In these instances there is a tendency for some bankers to reach for yields with the consequent sacrifice of proper maturity spacing.

With the bond portfolio accounting for about 35 per cent of the total assets of the banks of the nation and for about 25 per cent of their income, the comments and recommendations of the supervisory authorities, as well as their criticisms, should be carefully reviewed. Insofar as bankers heed their helpful suggestions, to that extent will management of bond accounts be strengthened. In so doing, bankers will be managing their banks more competently, and so discharging their first responsibility more completely.

SUGGESTED READINGS

AMERICAN BANKERS ASSOCIATION, Economic Policy Commission, *The Effects of Federal Reserve Policies, Monetary Study No. 4,* New York, American Bankers Association, 1954.

————, *The Effects of Treasury Operations, Monetary Study No. 5,* New York, American Bankers Association, 1954.

ATKINS, P. M., *Bank Bond Investment and Secondary Reserve Management,* Boston, Bankers' Publishing Company, 1940.

BADGER, RALPH E. and GUTHMANN, HARRY G., *Investment Principles and Practices,* New York, Prentice-Hall, Inc., 1951.

GRAHAM, BENJAMIN and DODD, DAVID L., *Security Analysis; Principles and Technique,* New York, McGraw-Hill Book Company, Inc., 1951.

SAUVAIN, HARRY C., *Investment Management,* New York, Prentice-Hall, Inc., 1953.

WILKINSON, J. HARVEY, *Investment Policies for Commercial Banks,* New York, Harper & Brothers, 1938.

WOOSTER, J. W., JR., *Bankers' Handbook of Bond Investment,* New York, Harper & Brothers, 1939.

V

CAPITAL, SURPLUS, AND RESERVES

THE ability or inability of a bank to absorb losses of any kind is limited by the relative size of the bank's capital, surplus, and reserves. The current and growing interest in the relative size of a bank's capital account is a result of the extraordinary growth in deposits and in loan and investment portfolios of the banking system, especially in the postwar years, as compared to the increase in the capital accounts.

CAPITAL GROWTH AND RATIOS

As shown in Table 11, bank deposits of the member banks of the Federal Reserve System, for example, have increased about four times from $33.7 billion in 1929 to $141 billion as of the end of 1954, whereas the capital accounts of member banks have about doubled from $6.7 billion as of the end of 1929 to $12.2 billion at the end of 1954. Similarly contrasting, loans and investments almost quadrupled from $35.9 billion in 1929 to $132 billion as of December 31, 1954.

In other words, although total capital accounts of the banks have increased, loans and investments and total deposits have grown faster. As a consequence, there has been a marked decline in bank capital in relation to deposits, loans, and investments as shown in Table 11 and as illustrated in Chart I. As of December 31, 1954, the capital to loan and investment ratio declined to 9.3 per cent from a ratio of 18.7 per cent in 1929. The ratio of capital to deposits traced

TABLE 11. PRINCIPAL ASSETS AND LIABILITIES OF MEMBER BANKS
(*Selected Years*)

Years as of end of December	Total Loans and Investments (*$ Millions*)	Total Deposits^a (*$ Millions*)	Total Capital Accounts (*$ Millions*)	Capital to Loans and Investments (*Per Cent*)	Capital to Deposits (*Per Cent*)
1929	35,934	33,671	6,709	18.7	19.9
1930	34,860	32,264	6,593	18.9	20.4
1935	29,985	32,159	5,145	17.2	16.0
1940	37,126	46,007	5,698	15.3	12.4
1945	107,183	116,030	7,589	7.1	6.5
1950	107,424	119,641	9,695	9.0	8.1
1954	131,602	141,269	12,210	9.3	8.6

SOURCE: Board of Governors, *Banking and Monetary Statistics* figures through 1940; and *Federal Reserve Bulletins* for subsequent years.
^a Except interbank.

a similar pattern from a ratio of almost 20 per cent in 1929 to about 9 per cent as of the end of December 1954. Both ratios have recovered slightly from the low points reached in the mid 1940's, as banks added to their capital accounts at an accelerated rate during the postwar years.

This decline in capital ratios has been true despite conservative dividend policies and the retention of a large portion of earnings to build capital accounts, as shown in Table 12. In other words, earnings have not been sufficient, primarily because of high taxes, to build adequate capital accounts. Basically, however, the need for larger capital accounts results from the fact that deposits and loans and investments have increased more rapidly than have retained

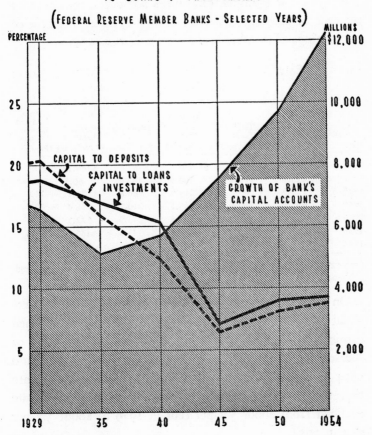

CHART I

TOTAL CAPITAL ACCOUNTS AND THE RATIOS OF
CAPITAL TO DEPOSITS AND
TO LOANS & INVESTMENTS

(FEDERAL RESERVE MEMBER BANKS - SELECTED YEARS)

earnings which have been added to capital accounts. As was pointed out above, this has weakened the ratio of capital to deposits and also the ratio of capital to loans and investments.

In 1929, for example, total taxes accounted for about 17 per cent of earnings, whereas, during 1954, 42 per cent of the earnings of member banks were paid out in taxes.

TABLE 12. EARNINGS, TAXES AND DIVIDENDS OF MEMBER BANKS
(Selected Years)

Year	Earnings Before Taxes *($ Millions)*	Total Taxes *($ Millions)*	Profits After Taxes *($ Millions)*	Dividends Paid *($ Millions)*	Retained Earnings *($ Millions)*	Ratio Retained Earnings to Profits *(Per Cent)*
1929	$ 668.9	$112.5	$ 556.5	$387.4	$169.1	30.4
1930	419.9	113.4	306.5	367.0	60.5	——
1935	275.5	63.7	211.9	186.8	25.1	11.8
1940	449.5	100.4	349.1	210.5	138.6	39.7
1945	1,058.5	270.1	788.4	245.9	542.5	68.8
1950	1,149.9	369.1	780.8	345.5	435.3	55.8
1954	1,900.3	804.2	1,096.1	456.1	640.0	58.4

SOURCE: Board of Governors, *Banking and Monetary Statistics* figures through 1940; and *Federal Reserve Bulletins* for subsequent years.

On the other hand, earnings before taxes in 1954 were about three times what they were in 1929, whereas retained earnings increased nearly fourfold. This was possible of course because total dividend payments between 1929 and 1954 increased only slightly. When dividend payments are expressed as a percentage of total capital accounts, the rate declined from about 5.8 per cent in 1929 to about 3.7 per cent in 1954.

NEED FOR INCREASED CAPITAL

Banks need further to strengthen their capital accounts not only in order to be able to absorb losses during periods of stress but perhaps even more importantly to be able to provide credit in adequate amounts when it is needed most. Equally important, bankers need to build their capital accounts in order to take care of the expanded credit needs of their customers because of the growth of the economy. A bank in a growing community and with growing businesses must have a growing capital structure if it is to meet the increasing credit requirements of its customers and the community. The management of every bank should carefully analyze its risks, determine its capital requirements, and work out an adequate and definite program for increasing its capital, surplus, and reserves.[1]

It cannot be overemphasized that we must continue to play our historic role as suppliers of credit and play it well, during relatively prosperous times as well as during other periods. This not only requires a kind of financial statesmanship; it also requires that our banks have adequate capital accounts if these responsibilities are to be adequately and fully discharged. Anything less and we fail in our obligations to our stockholders, our depositors, and our communities. Moreover, we fail properly to support our economic system of private enterprise and individual initiative. If we fail, either because we lack the courage or the capital, there will be suggestions that government agencies do the task, and we shall encourage the growth and expansion of other types of private lending agencies.

It is the responsibility of the banker therefore to see that

---

[1] For a more complete discussion see Gaylord A. Freeman, Jr., *The Problems of Adequate Bank Capital*, an analysis prepared for the Illinois Bankers' Association in 1952.

his bank has adequate capital to absorb the losses that inevitably occur in the day-to-day business of extending credit, and also as a result of the fluctuations of the restless business cycle. A banker must strengthen his capital accounts during periods of prosperity well in advance of any possible business recession. Since additional capital probably will not be available during periods of declining economic activity, a bank may be obliged to reduce its loans just at a time when the entire economy needs an expansion rather than a contraction of credit.

Newer banks especially have experienced increases in loan volume far in excess of their capital growth. Such banks need more capital immediately, and with continued growth in the demand for loans many more banks will need additional capital. The banker must constantly realize that if his capital is not keeping pace with the growth of industries and the community he serves, his bank may be handicapped because of the limited amount it can loan to its largest and frequently best accounts. In addition, this inability to extend credit in sufficiently large amounts to satisfy the requirements of borrowers could lead ultimately to a decline in the importance of banks as suppliers of credit, and the substitution of other lenders able and willing to meet the needs of sound borrowers.

Because of the growing significance of the capital accounts to competent bank management, the questionnaire which was sent to the national and state supervisory authorities included a section devoted to bank capital, surplus, and reserves. The examiners were asked for their views in general on capital, surplus, reserves, and earnings. They were asked, in particular, if earnings, in their opinion, were adequate to build strong capital and surplus accounts? Did the banks, under their jurisdiction, have satisfactory programs for building their capital accounts? Based on their unique experience in examining these banks annually, did they believe that adequate provision was being made for losses and other contingencies?

EARNINGS ARE ADEQUATE

In general, most of the forty-six supervisory agencies responding to the questionnaire felt that earnings are adequate to build strong capital, surplus, and reserve accounts and that satisfactory programs for building these accounts are in effect.

More specifically, about three out of four of the agencies were in agreement with the following reply: "We conclude, on an over-all picture, that banks are earning and retaining sufficient funds reasonably to fortify themselves with capital buffer. There are individual cases," the same report continued, "wherein retained earnings are not keeping pace with the expansion in business. These are isolated cases, but the large majority of them have recognized the need of additional capital strength and have sold new shares, with gratifying response."

However, there were strong exceptions to this viewpoint. Among the 25 per cent of the examining agencies who were of the opinion that earnings are not sufficient and that as a consequence capital, surplus, and reserve accounts are not keeping pace with the growth in deposits, frequent mention was made that two problems are involved. One problem is that because of the relatively low yields on loans and investments and the high tax rates many banks are precluded from increasing capital from earnings.

HIGH TAX RATES

One examiner expressed it this way, "Although gross earnings have been extremely high, the net after taxes has been insufficient to maintain a strong capital structure. Deposits have increased so rapidly that it has been necessary, in some instances, to sell additional stock." Increased operating expenses were cited as another factor which has retarded capital expansion during the prosperous postwar years.

Another reply emphasizing earnings read that they "are not sufficient under the present tax structure to keep pace with the ever-increasing risk assets as well as the continued increase of deposits."

One supervisory authority replied at length on the inadequacy of earnings in general "to build sufficiently strong capital and surplus accounts without the aid of capital stock investment. The need for more capital investment has resulted from the great expansion in loans and the security investments of a risk type, and also because in many situations current earnings are not sufficient to maintain capital in adequate volume. It should, of course, be noted," the reply continued, "that many banking institutions with strong capitalizations have had earnings of sufficient volume to maintain capital in appropriate relation to risk assets."

ABSENCE OF PLAN FOR INCREASING CAPITAL

The second problem involved in the lack of proportionate growth of capital accounts, mentioned by about one out of every four replying to the survey, was that programs for building capital, surplus, and reserve accounts frequently are not clearly and definitely outlined and followed. "Very few programs for building capital and surplus accounts are found," according to one reply. It is said to be a "hit or miss" proposition rather than a carefully planned program for building the capital accounts.

One national agency summarized the situation this way: "There is one general observation to be made on the question of satisfactory programs for building capital, surplus, and reserves. Frequently, bank management seeks to maintain or even increase the rate of dividends at the expense of any set goal or program for capital increase from a fixed proportion of earnings."

DIVIDEND POLICIES

There were several additional comments regarding dividend policies. Some banks have a tendency to subordinate the need for increased capital to the insistence of directors and stockholders for substantial dividend disbursements. One examiner bluntly reported, "This is always a bone of contention with boards of directors. Too many directors and stockholders are much more interested in large dividends."

A supervisor from a predominantly agricultural state in commenting on the same subject wrote that "the individual banks in our state have adequate capital and surplus for the protection of their depositors, and we are happy to say that we have been successful in impressing upon the management of our rural banks the necessity for conserving income to supplement their capital structure for any contingencies which may confront them in the future, instead of paying out exorbitant cash dividends to their stockholders."

Another reply summarized the problem with the statement, "A great amount of the time of our commercial bank division is devoted to emphasis on adequate capital. The tremendous growth enjoyed by most banking institutions in the last decade has resulted in numerous instances where capital strengthening has become necessary. Strong pressure is exerted to convince the directors of our banks of the need for affirmative action. There remain many banks, however, which in the opinion of this department do not have adequate capital positions. Usually, these are rapidly growing institutions who find it difficult to maintain strong capital and surplus accounts out of earnings."

On the other hand, another national agency remarked that "banks in general are aware of the need for capital funds in sufficient volume to protect the interest of depositors, and considerable progress has been made by bankers in recent years in building up under-capitalized institutions."

INTEREST PAID ON SAVINGS

A number of the supervisory authorities, when independently answering this portion of the questionnaire, expressed a common concern about banks increasing the rate of interest paid on time and savings deposits. One examiner commenting on the subject wrote that this "current trend among banks— of increasing the interest paid on time and savings accounts —is a matter of concern since this item presently accounts for about 20 per cent of operating expenses and over 13 per cent of gross earnings. We feel," the reply continued, "that the competition from building and loan associations is forcing many banks into ill-advised programs in regard to payment of interest. We feel that as an offset to increased interest expense some banks may effect economies in operations inconsistent with good practice." The agency replying to the questionnaire went on to describe one bank that was doubling its interest on time deposits to meet local competition. "On the basis of net earnings for 1953," the reply continued, "this would just about absorb all of its net operating profits unless earnings can be increased to absorb all or part of the increased interest being paid. Conservatism in this respect cannot be overemphasized."

LOSS RESERVES

Reserves for losses and contingencies are related to the adequacy of capital and surplus accounts. Here, again, better than two-thirds of the replies concluded that such reserve accounts are adequate, although a number cautioned that there appears to be little correlation between the provision for loan losses and the current loss experience of individual banks. Also, it was frequently pointed out that any conclusion is questionable which states that total reserves for all banks in a certain jurisdiction are adequate but fails to analyze the reserve needs of each individual bank based on the historical record over many years.

SUMMARY

In summary, the general opinion was:

First, earnings are in most cases sufficient to build strong capital accounts.

Second, progress is being made in strengthening the capital accounts of banks.

Third, the obstacles to strengthening the capital accounts of banks are the relatively low yields on loans and investments, high tax rates, and the lack of a clearly defined capital expansion program.

The subject of building adequate capital, surplus, and reserves is of such far-reaching importance to the depositor, the borrower, the stockholder, and the community that it should constantly be in the forefront of the objectives of good bank management.

SUGGESTED READINGS

ALDRICH, WINTHROP W., *Economic Significance of Postwar Changes in Commercial Bank Portfolio,* An Address Delivered Before the 52nd Annual Convention of the New York State Bankers Association, January 4, 1948.

AMERICAN BANKERS ASSOCIATION, Research Council, *The Adequacy of a Bank's Capital Funds* (A Statement of Principles), New York, American Bankers Association, 1954.

COOKE, HELEN J. MELLON, "Significance of Bank Capital Ratios," *Journal of Political Economy,* Vol. 57, No. 1 (February 1949).

FEDERAL DEPOSIT INSURANCE CORPORATION, *Assets, Liabilities and Capital Accounts: Capital and Other Ratios of Commercial and Mutual Savings Banks,* (semi-annually), Washington.

FEDERAL RESERVE BANK OF CHICAGO, "Facts About Bank Capital," *Business Conditions,* March 1952.

FREEMAN, GAYLORD A., JR., *The Problems of Adequate Bank Capital,* an analysis prepared for the Illinois Bankers' Association, The First National Bank of Chicago, 1952.

INSTITUTE OF INTERNATIONAL FINANCE OF NEW YORK UNIVERSITY, *Ratio of Capital Funds to Deposits of Commercial Banks in the United States*, Bulletin No. 112 (October 14, 1940), Institute of International Finance of New York University.

NEW YORK STATE BANKERS ASSOCIATION, Committee on Risk Asset Ratio Study, *Risk Asset Ratio Study*, New York State Bankers Association, 1952.

ROBINSON, ROLAND I., "Bank Capital and Dividend Policies," *Harvard Business Review*, Vol. 26, No. 4 (July 1948).

———, "The Capital-Deposit Ratio in Banking Supervision," *Journal of Political Economy*, Vol. 49, No. 1 (February 1941).

RYAN, JOHN, "Bank Capital and Size and Location of Banks," *Journal of Business*, Vol. 25, No. 4 (October 1952).

SMITH, T. and HENGREN, R., "Bank Capital: The Problem Restated," *Journal of Political Economy*, Vol. 55, No. 6 (December 1947).

WILLIS, J. BROOKE, *The Functions of the Commercial Banking System*, Morningside Heights, New York, King's Crown Press, 1943.

VI

ACCOUNTING, INTERNAL CONTROL, AND TAXES

B ANKS are institutions that deal with money. Their business is finance, their stock in trade is currency and credit. As a consquence, banks are a kind of huge accounting machine transferring the ownership of money and credit and keeping a record of such transfers. It follows, therefore, that one of the principal responsibilities of bank management is accounting and the related functions of auditing and internal control, that is, the protection of the assets of the bank against loss arising from the factor of human frailty.[1]

Banking history bears out the necessity for audit control and supervision in the handling of money and its equivalent. Frailties of human beings entrusted with the property of others must be accepted as an ever-present hazard. Some fidelity insurance authorities, for example, have estimated

---

[1] More specifically, the National Association of Bank Auditors and Comptrollers defines accounting as "the science which treats of the systematic record; 'auditing' is the art of reviewing the work incidental to the records. 'Control' means to check or regulate, whereas audit means a formal or official authentication of accounts."

SOURCE: *NABAC Manual, Bank Accounting, Auditing and Operation*— Compiled and published by The National Association of Bank Auditors and Comptrollers, page 111.

that undiscovered losses due to misappropriation of bank assets and income amount to $10 million.

The audit function is the principal deterrent to defalcations. Auditing, however, as described by the National Association of Bank Auditors and Comptrollers, is not just being an accounting policeman, but includes by its nature good accounting and operating procedures. In other words, the auditing responsibility is to see that the funds of the bank and its customers, as well as all other valuables for which the bank has responsibility, are properly accounted for and adequately protected.

AUDITING—A MANAGEMENT RESPONSIBILITY

Despite this fact, however, auditing often is not recognized as an important management function and responsibility. The National Association of Bank Auditors and Comptrollers has estimated that only about 1000 banks have full time auditors and perhaps another 500 banks have a partial audit program. As a consequence, some 13,000 banks are without an adequate auditing program. This means that 90 per cent of the banks in the United States are subject to loss by not having complete preventive measures.

It therefore becomes a major responsibility of the executive officers and directors to recognize and to appreciate the serious importance of the accounting and audit functions and to exercise their authority by requiring a reasonable control program.

A portion of the questionnaire on bank management, therefore, included a section on accounting, auditing, and related problems. The examiners were asked to appraise bank accounting systems, and, secondly, to comment on audit and control procedures.

The great majority of the replies, almost 70 per cent, reported that accounting systems are adequate, but that audit controls are not too well established, although progress has been made in recent years. Many replies praised the American Bankers Association and the National Association of Bank Auditors and Comptrollers for their efforts to promote the use of audit control safeguards. In short, while accounting systems appear generally to be reasonably adequate, control or administration of them is frequently poor.

SIZE OF BANK A FACTOR

Most agencies, in answering the query on whether banks had audit programs in effect, administered either by a member of their staff or by an outside firm, said that the answer would depend on the size of the bank being considered. The most difficult problems on this aspect of management naturally arise in the smaller or medium-sized banks. The solution is not simple. These bankers contend that they cannot afford either to include an auditor on their staff or to employ the services of an outside auditing firm. Most of the larger banks on the other hand cannot afford to be without a competent auditing staff and usually have able personnel. Cost being the primary consideration of the small bank, a number of examining agencies suggested that more thought should be given to a partial audit system on a continuing basis which would complement the supervisory examination.

A national agency in commenting on accounting systems wrote as follows: "The more serious deficiencies in account-

ing and internal controls exist principally in the small or medium-sized banks. There has been, and still is, a marked laxity
in this important function and much work needs to be done."

The same agency in commenting on the failure of a bank
to have an auditor or to hire an outside auditing firm wrote,
"The average country bank does not feel that it can afford to
have a full time auditor . . . and very few do. This office
stresses the need of comprehensive examinations by the directors in banks of this category and recommends the employment of an outside auditor in conjunction therewith, especially
when members of the examining committee are not acquainted with the principles of good accounting and control."

Another supervisor described the lack of audit programs
in banks as "the most neglected and most needy of attention
on the part of bank management. The field is still too fertile
for the embezzler." The report went on to describe other benefits that would result from regular audits, "We believe that
even the smallest bank would benefit by an outside audit and
survey of its operations, not only for the purpose of elimi-
nating possible avenues of embezzlement and theft, but for
cost purposes as well."

The same report concluded with perhaps the even more
significant comment that "unless bank management voluntar-
ily improves its own accounting and auditing procedures and
systems, the entire bank examination procedure may soon
have to be revised to include more auditing aspects."

On the other hand, a number mentioned the "growing
interest prevalent among our banks respecting some type of
audit program." However, one state official observed, "Some
banks which should be able to afford and should have a regu-

larly employed auditor, with proper authority and responsibility, have not seen fit to engage one."

A number of replies also mentioned that the boards of directors in many of the small unit banks with inadequate auditing and control systems were reluctant to follow supervisory urging on this important management function. One report said that "this resistance to the examiners' suggestions were on the basis of the cost of installing such auditing and internal controls."

The same state agency wrote that their "own studies have led us to believe that banks with resources of about $10 million should have resident full time auditors, while those with resources below that figure should avail themselves of the services of outside accountants. Each year more and more of them take steps to improve their practices in these aspects," the report continued. "There is a hard core of usually well-run small banks which will not adopt recommended systems, usually because of the cost."

A PROPOSAL

In a similar vein, another supervisor noted that while it is rare for banks under $10 million to have a full-fledged auditor or outside firm responsible to the board of directors because of the cost, "it is surprising that more thought has not been given to a partial audit system on a continuing basis which would complement the supervisory examination. In our opinion," the report concluded, "the earnings of banks above $4 million in assets should support the expense of an auditor."

In contrast, several examiners said that internal audit systems often are inadequate, especially in the smaller banks, because of the "many and diverse additional duties placed on the bank auditor."

Still other replies mentioned that the bank auditor, at times, "is a secondary position without proper consideration given as to caliber and responsibility. There is, however, evidence of improvement. Banks," the reply added, "have been slow to recognize the value of an audit by a firm of public accountants either periodically or on a continuing basis as a supplement to the internal audit system or in substitution thereof, when the internal audit setup is inadequate or nonexistent. The pure audit functions of checking daily transactions, income, and expense on a periodic basis, and the verifications of deposits and of assets need more emphasis."

On the other hand, some authorities cautioned that frequently "outside auditing firms do not prove satisfactory because of a general lack of familiarity with banking procedures."

OBSTACLES TO AUDIT PROGRAMS

While there are many reasons causing the deficiency of the audit programs found in some country banks, the primary reason is "insufficient personnel which makes impossible the setting up of a satisfactory internal system of checks and balances among the operating personnel. We have continually brought this fact before the directorates of our country banks," the report continued, "alerting them to the exposures which exist in their banks." This absence of suitable accounting controls obviously does not exist by the design of management, but because of "the lack of funds and personnel to permit such a program to be set up in their banks. In the absence of these programs," the report continued, "we have continually requested the directorates to have their banks audited by outside certified public accountants, and we are happy to state that we have received reasonable cooperation by many of the country banks' directorates in this field." Typical of many replies was the hopeful conclusion of this same report "that the program of the National Association of Bank Auditors and Comptrollers which is now being presented to the small banks of the country will open an avenue which will ultimately provide some program at a cost figure which the country banks can meet, and which will permit them to have an accounting system and auditing program that will afford the bank reasonable protection."

TAXES AND REPORTS TO MANAGEMENT

Frequently another responsibility of the accounting and auditing function is the matter of taxes. Consequently, the examiners were asked to comment on the knowledge which bankers have of tax problems.

Most of the replies indicated that bankers are tax conscious, and keep themselves well informed on tax matters in various ways including the employment of tax consultants or counselors.

To the query as to the adequacy of the reports to management and the Board of Directors, only eight of the forty-six agencies replying to the questionnaire were of the opinion that the reports were not sufficient. However, many added that "there is much still to be done in convincing management of the necessity for adequate reports to directors." This criticism, interestingly enough, was not limited to the smaller banks. One supervisory agency expressed it this way: "The reports furnished to directors in the smaller banks and to management and directors of the larger ones are often inadequate."

"The reports," another observed, "range from the most elaborate presentation to those of utmost simplicity. Most organizations make an effort to keep the management fully informed of actions taken by the bank. The means of transmitting such information," it was noted, however, "are varied and in some institutions it is done largely on an oral basis."

INSURANCE

The survey on bank management also asked if the insurance of banks was sufficient to cover possible losses. The replies, almost unanimous, were that insurance coverage of banks was adequate to cover possible losses. Most of them also indicated that banks generally follow the recommendations of the American Bankers Association Protective Committee. However, several cautioned that while amounts appear adequate now, no one is competent to say if in fact they will be under all contingencies.

SUMMARY

Seven out of ten of the replies reported that while accounting systems are satisfactory, auditing controls in many banks could be improved. Auditing systems and methods should be constantly reviewed; such protective devices as may be necessary to safeguard against irregularities should be established.

The consensus was that reports to senior officials and directors are comprehensive, though a number of bank examiners felt that management could be kept better informed.

Most of the replies indicated that the bankers were keeping themselves well advised on taxes, either by having a tax specialist in the bank, or by retaining a tax consultant.

The absence of proper auditing programs subjects a bank to greater risk of loss than would be necessary if adequate internal control arrangements were in force. Responsibility for this management function rests squarely on the shoulders of the directors and the executive officers of the bank.

SUGGESTED READINGS

AMERICAN BANKERS ASSOCIATION, Bank Management Commission, *A Guide for Spot Check Audit Control,* Bank Management Publication No. 134, New York, American Bankers Association, 1954.

———, Country Bank Operations Commission and the Insurance and Protective Commission, *How to Set Up an Audit Program in the Smaller Bank,* New York, American Bankers Association, 1953.

MERTZ, HARRY E., *Internal Safeguards for Country Banks,* Chicago, The National Association of Bank Auditors and Comptrollers, 1953.

THE NATIONAL ASSOCIATION OF BANK AUDITORS AND COMPTROLLERS, Commercial Operations Commission, *Commercial Proof Department Operations,* Chicago, The National Association of Bank Auditors and Comptrollers, 1955.

———, Committee on Duties and Responsibilities of a Bank Auditor and Comptroller, *Duties and Responsibilities of a Bank Auditor and/or Comptroller* (a survey), Chicago, The National Association of Bank Auditors and Comptrollers, 1951.

————, Committee on Problems of Smaller Banks, *Audit Schedule Control Book,* Chicago, The National Association of Bank Auditors and Comptrollers, 1949.

————, *NABAC Manual: Bank Accounting, Auditing and Operation,* Chicago, The National Association of Bank Auditors and Comptrollers, 1951.

————, The Research Committee, *Audit Program for the Smaller Bank,* Chicago, The National Association of Bank Auditors and Comptrollers, 1950.

————, The Research Committee, *The Commercial Bookkeeping Department* (a survey), Chicago, The National Association of Bank Auditors and Comptrollers, 1949.

————, The Trust Commission, *Audit Schedule for Smaller Trust Department,* Chicago, The National Association of Bank Auditors and Comptrollers, 1953.

PRATT, LESTER A., "Still Better Audit Control," *United States Investor,* Vol. 63, No. 44 (November 1, 1952).

VOGEL, ALVIN J., *Teller Operating Procedure,* Chicago, The National Association of Bank Auditors and Comptrollers, 1948.

VII

PERSONNEL TRAINING
AND SUCCESSOR MANAGEMENT

WALTER LIPPMANN once observed, "The test of a leader is that he leaves behind him in other men the conviction and the will to carry on. . . . The genius of a good leader is to leave behind him a situation which common sense, without the grace of genius, can deal with successfully." These words have significance for banking leaders of today in their efforts to perpetuate their organizations and serve their communities.

The Comptroller of the Currency and many state banking authorities grant perpetual charters to banks. This theoretically insures the continuous operation of the bank in the community and thus lends stability to the economy.

To fulfill their obligations to their depositors, stockholders, and the community, those who manage our banks must not only meet the day-to-day financial needs of their customers but also must prepare their institutions for future operations as well. To do this management must, despite past success, recognize clearly that they have only a temporary tenure of office within the long history of their organizations. In addition, they should anticipate the continued growth of their

86

banks. Bank management should understand fully that one of the results of truly successful leadership is the development of another successful management team. Developing strong leadership for the years ahead is no less important than building adequate capital, surplus, and reserves.

DEMAND FOR BANK PERSONNEL

In the postwar years, the problem of personnel development and successor management in banks has become more acute for a number of reasons. First, there has been a substantial growth in the size of banks and in the number of branches. Since 1936, for example, the total assets of member banks of the Federal Reserve System have increased 253 per cent with loans increasing more than 300 per cent. Capital accounts have more than doubled, and total deposits are up 291 per cent. The number of member banks during this period increased 4 per cent and the number of branches and additional offices operated by these institutions increased from 2379 to 4787 units, an increase of over 100 per cent.

A second factor contributing to the personnel and successor management problem which is of major concern to banking leaders has been the increase in the number and variety of services offered by banks. In the last two decades, for example, consumer installment credit has grown significantly from $2.7 billion in 1935 to about $24.9 billion as of June 1955. This form of credit is now extended by many thousands of banks. Term loans, which have also developed in relatively recent years, are now an important credit form or technique in the larger American banks. The demand for trust services, especially pension and profit sharing trusts, has increased.

These are but a few of the new and growing services provided by banks which have required additional specialized bank personnel.

A third factor in aggravating the successor management

TABLE 13. NUMBER OF BANKS AND BRANCHES, TOTAL ASSETS, LOANS AND DISCOUNTS, DEPOSITS, AND CAPITAL FOR MEMBER BANKS OF FEDERAL RESERVE SYSTEM
(*Selected Years*)

Year	Number Banks	Number of Branches	Total Assets (*$ Millions*)	Loans and Discounts (*Including Overdrafts*) (*$ Millions*)	Deposits[a] (*$ Millions*)	Capital (*$ Millions*)
1936	6,376	2,379	48,708	13,360	35,892	5,275
1940	6,486	2,541	62,658	15,321	46,007	5,698
1945	6,884	2,909	138,304	22,775	116,030	7,589
1950	6,873	3,589	144,660	44,705	119,641	9,695
1953	6,743	4,398	163,983	57,762	134,994	11,316
1954	6,660	4,787	172,242	60,250	141,269	12,210

SOURCE: Board of Governors, *Federal Reserve Bulletins.*
[a] Except interbank.

problem is that the talents required of bank executives have greatly increased in recent years as the economy in which banks must operate has become increasingly complex. To cite one example, the role of the Federal Reserve System, our central bank, has become one of major proportions, its decisions and activities greatly influencing the economy and thus exerting an impact on the individual bank's operations.

The size and complexity of the operations of many of our borrowing customers have also increased so that bank officers are often dealing with much larger individual business loans. Furthermore, we are operating in an economy where the nation has a Federal debt of over $275 billion and where

Federal Government securities constitute approximately 34 per cent of Federal Reserve member banks' earning assets. We need a much more thorough understanding of fiscal problems, debt management, and Federal budget problems than were required of bankers even as late as the 1920's and 1930's. With the United States having attained the financial leadership of the world, American bankers are confronted with the necessity for a far broader knowledge of banking, economic, fiscal, and monetary problems, both national and international, than were required at any time in the history of American banking.

As a consequence of these three factors, namely, the growth in the size of banks, the increase in bank services, and our complex financial and economic environment, bank management has come to realize that the problems of personnel development and successor management are growing increasingly difficult to solve. The bank executive of tomorrow must be one of broader vision, wider experience, and greater capabilities, requiring a good education and a higher degree of careful and intensive training.

Total bank personnel in the last twenty years has about doubled, while official staffs have increased only about 71 per cent. If the future growth of the banking system continues as in the past, we may expect the demand for bank executives to increase substantially. This demand is in addition to those required to replace present leaders as they retire and otherwise leave their responsibilities.

Bank management may find the supply of men available to staff these responsibilities decidedly limited because of the low birth rates of the early 1930's. In addition, the demand for the services of the existing supply of young men will be bid for by industry, government and the professions, all of whom have experienced more or less the same growth which has characterized banking.

To solve the problem of successor management, banks must attract to their business alert young men of high caliber by

TABLE 14. NUMBER OF PERSONNEL AND AMOUNT OF PAYROLLS
MEMBER BANKS OF FEDERAL RESERVE SYSTEM
(*Selected Years*)

Year	Total Personnel	Number of Officers	Number in Clerical Staff	Total Payrolls (*$ Millions*)	Officers' Salaries (*$ Millions*)	Clerical Salaries (*$ Millions*)
1936	181,302	31,880	149,422	351	135	216
1940	199,152	35,369	163,783	400	155	245
1945	247,363	39,903	207,460	579	208	371
1950	312,610	48,967	263,643	1,000	345	655
1953	370,611	54,639	315,972	1,371	447	924
1954	380,486	56,541	323,945	1,463	479	984

SOURCE: Board of Governors, *Federal Reserve Bulletins.*

offering them challenging opportunities and attractive remuneration, permitting each of them to develop to the highest degree of his ability.

To determine whether or not today's bank personnel policies are meeting the successor management problem, the following questions were included in the questionnaire which was sent to the national and state supervisory authorities:

1. Is there a failure to plan for continuing top management?

2. Is there a failure to train employees for their jobs?

3. Are salaries adequate for officers?

4. Are salaries adequate for employees?

BANKING'S BIGGEST PROBLEM

The agencies, responding independently, were in almost complete agreement that one of the biggest problems confronting bank management today is the matter of successor management. The overwhelming majority, forty-three out of the forty-six replies received, expressed this view. One frankly stated, "Failure on the part of top management and directors to provide for management replacements or reserves is one of the most serious weaknesses in our present banking system, if not the most serious. We find that lack of training programs, lack of proper salary advancement programs, and the general lack of attention to the entire subject of personnel may lead to a lessening of the quality of service to customers and a deterioration in employee morale and related problems."

The authorities noted that the problem of successor management has existed for a long period. Despite the fact that they have informed management of the need for replacements and reserves of trained men some banks have not attempted to meet the need.

One state banking authority acknowledged, "I have served as superintendent in this state for nearly fifteen years and feel that my greatest disappointment has been my inability to persuade the managing officers and the directors that they should train competent young men to step into their shoes when the time comes. They will promise and admit that they should do it, but keep putting off the day to turn over some responsibility to the younger officers."

"In the average small independent bank," still another wrote, "there is failure to plan for continuing top management for at least two reasons. One is the tremendous difficulty in finding capable management in the first place, and the other is the fact that the present old management in many cases will not give up. That is, the management will not train employees to fill their jobs and will not delegate responsibility so that an employee can be trained to fill the next job above."

ONE-MAN BANKS

The establishment of a program of management development is difficult, especially in "one-man" banks. This is due in some cases to the fact that the income of the bank may not allow any extensive training period and, in other cases, to the fact that top management just will not tolerate the installation of a replacement plan. The resulting lack of experienced leadership if the top executive unexpectedly dies or is incapacitated may have a serious effect on the bank.

In commenting on the "one-man" bank situation and the problem it frequently engenders, one examiner wrote as follows: "We have many cases ... where there is and has been a failure to plan for continuing top management. I refer to this situation as a 'one-man bank.' It is surprising to learn how many times we have been aware that in a particular institution only one officer is carrying on the executive affairs of the bank. In many cases, there are junior officers who would have considerable ability to take over, if necessary, if the executive officer would take the time to give them the benefit of his years of experience. In too many institutions of small and medium size, the employees and junior officers are too limited in the duties they are permitted to perform and in the responsibilities assigned to them. I think that this has been the cause of many mergers and voluntary liquidation of banking institutions."

One agency replying to the questionnaire included the following case from its files, illustrating the difficulties resulting from a failure to provide for successor management. The case involved a bank chartered shortly after World War II, in a city with a population of about 9000. "The father of the present president was the organizer of the bank and was a sound banker even though he was 'the bank.' His health failed and he brought his son in to run the business. The father shortly lost his memory. The competition is a branch of one of the [big city] banks and is conservative." According to the reply, "This son was not prepared for the position assumed and has what the examiner terms 'a dummy board of directors.' The earnings have been good, but losses have been four times the average. Credit is extended in a loose manner in unsound risk loans without a sound repayment policy. No dividends are being paid, and the father and son own 70 per cent of the stock." The deteriorating situation has also affected the employees who "are not happy as they say they are not told what their duties are and then are criticized for not having done some other task."

Another example of "too little, too late" was reported. It almost resulted in depriving the community of the bank's services. "The president of the bank was an old, sick man. His cashier was old and in bad health. The only other persons in the bank were two inexperienced girl bookkeepers. This is a one million dollar bank. The president owned 88 per cent of the capital stock, the cashier owned 6 per cent, and three other individuals owned 2 per cent each. All five were directors. The president died suddenly. The cashier called this office and said that the bank would have to have someone to operate it as he was sick and had to go to the hospital. Before someone was found to take over, the bank operated several days with only four directors [which is illegal] with most of the stock tied up in an estate and none available for a fifth director." It began to look as though it would be necessary to "close the bank and liquidate it, depriving the community of banking services. However, through much work and effort it was finally successfully worked out." The report concluded with the opinion that "this condition should not have arisen had the president just looked down the road a little farther."

The following reasons, according to a review of the replies to the questionnaire, account for the present apparent lack of bank personnel of management caliber:

First, the general lack of attention by executive officers and directors to this problem.

Second, the difficulty of finding good junior officers.

Third, the problem of offering adequate salaries.

Fourth, the failure of bank officials to delegate authority.

Fifth, related to the last reason, the failure of bank management to offer challenging and stimulating responsibilities in an attempt to attract and retain promising young men.

GROWTH IN SALARIES

A pervasive factor in any program of management and personnel development is that of salaries. In general, bank salaries may have been lower than those paid in some types of industries, but for 1953 the average salary of bank employees, including officers and clerks, was 6 per cent above the average salary of all workers, including executive, supervisory, and skilled and unskilled labor, in all industries in the United States.

Statistics indicate that banks have been attempting to solve the salary problem and have made significant strides forward. The annual payroll of member banks of the Federal Reserve System during the period of 1936 through 1953 has increased 290 per cent, with that for officers increasing 231 per cent and that for employees 328 per cent. The average salary for bank officials and bank staff personnel has increased 93 per cent and 102 per cent respectively during this period as compared with a 203 per cent increase in the average for all industry in the United States. However, there is perhaps in most banks greater job security than prevails for the average employee in business.

ADJUSTMENT OF SALARY SCALES

In commenting on the subject of salaries paid bank personnel one examining agency stated, "Much progress has been made by the banking institutions in adjusting their salary scales so that officers will receive adequate compensation, sufficient to keep them in the banking business and from entering other fields of business endeavor. Again, in the smaller institutions this problem has not been solved as well as in the medium-sized and larger institutions. Salaries for employees have also been receiving careful consideration from management during the last several years. It has been difficult to attract younger men to the field of banking. I believe that bankers generally are becoming aware of the necessity of paying adequate salaries in order to obtain the services of younger men with a view toward training them for a banking career."

INVESTING IN MANAGEMENT POTENTIAL

Frequently mentioned was the need for pension plans and fringe benefits to keep the turnover of personnel down. As one examiner remarked, "In most cases we feel that the salaries of officers are reasonably adequate, but many ... banks find it difficult to pay salaries sufficiently attractive to retain well qualified officers, who consequently shift to better paying positions. Much of the turnover in bank personnel is due to the inadequacy of salaries or the lack of fringe benefits or pension plans. Employment in other fields is very frequently more attractive due to higher salaries and greater opportunity for advancement." The unwillingness of management to face squarely the problem of executive training and succession is responsible for the loss of capable officers who could, if properly compensated, be retained to advantage by their banks.

"The 'prestige' formerly associated with employment in the banking field," the same reply continued, "is no longer a consideration to most young people in the selection of banking as a career. Banks could do much to relieve their personnel problems by improving their salary scale and by providing other benefits to compete with industry, particularly in the large communities. Country banks are probably less subject to this competition."

One examiner wrote, "At the risk of too general an observation, it might be said that banks pay their employees adequately for their immediate job performance, but frequently neglect to add the necessary amount to the salary which could be looked upon as a proper investment in potential management material, assuming such potential exists or needs to be attracted."

The figures cited above indicate that bank management has recognized the need of good salaries as one means to help insure a continuing supply of capable officers. Many, however, have not applied adequate methods for the development of men with potential. Despite the fact that the banking industry long ago recognized the need for formal training, little has been done to develop practical internal programs of personnel and executive development. Thirty of the forty-six examining agencies reported that the banks under their jurisdiction did not properly train employees for their jobs.

PERSONNEL DEVELOPMENT PROGRAM

The need for the development of officers within the organization requires the establishment of an objective method of employee selection and training. But no program or plan can be successful unless it receives the constant encouragement of the top executive group of the bank. At the outset, it should be recognized that the responsibility for personnel development rests squarely on the shoulders of every member of the official team. Only by providing inspired leadership and delegating authority and responsibility, the prerogatives of management, can the program be successful.

The first step in the development of an executive training program is the study of the bank and its present staff. A chart of organization may be drawn setting forth in clear terms the requirements of each managerial position. The chart of organization will vary from one bank to another and from one time to another due to the difference in the portfolios of earnings assets, the areas served, and developments over periods of time.

After the requirements of a job have been delineated, management may intelligently determine how well the job is being performed, and may also be able to appraise better those that are under consideration for eventual advancement to the position. With a plan of organization, and the requirements of each job clearly understood, management can more capably judge the strong and weak points of each individual on each job, and at what level he operates most efficiently. In this manner a specific plan of development may be drawn up for each person.

The true development of the individual is dependent, however, upon the delegation of authority in all levels, from the top of the organization down to the very bottom. Only in this way may the employee rise to the top level of his ability.

New situations and problems are arising constantly and these may be used as a means for broadening the individual's banking knowledge. The answers to these questions offer guides to the individual's progress. Did the employee solve this problem satisfactorily? How did he do it? Why did he do it in this particular way? How long did it take him? Is the solution of this problem consistent with his past solutions, or has some new element been injected? If some new element has been injected, is it an improvement? Only by answering these questions can management intelligently determine the individual's ability and knowledge. Only by solving the problems offered to him by management may the individual develop his skills.

FORMAL EDUCATION PROGRAM

Formal education and training in banking is also beneficial to the individual. The American Bankers Association and the various state banking associations have organized schools and developed programs in adult education to aid in the training of bank personnel.

The American Institute of Banking, the educational branch of the American Bankers Association, offers concentrated courses in banking, accounting, auditing, trusts, investments, economics, consumer credit, taxes, law, and real estate. The Institute, on January 1, 1955, had 275 chapters located in the principal cities across the nation and 142 study groups in smaller communities with a total of 112,138 members, or approximately 22 per cent of total bank employees. Enrollment in American Institute of Banking courses totaled 48,432 on January 1, 1955.

To provide for more advanced formal training in banking, the American Bankers Association organized The Graduate School of Banking at Rutgers University in 1935. The purpose of the school is to offer "a comprehensive approach to an advanced study of the various administrative problems in banking and trust institutions."[1]

Another institution to provide advanced training to bankers is The School of Banking established at the University of Wisconsin in 1945 and sponsored by the Central States

[1] Catalogue for the 1955 session, The Graduate School of Banking, American Bankers Association.

Conference[2] "to provide bankers an opportunity for advanced study and research in banking, economic, and monetary problems."[3]

There are two other schools of advanced adult banking education sponsored by various state banking associations: The School of Banking of the South at Louisiana State University and The Pacific Coast School of Banking at the University of Washington. There are also some worthwhile adult educational projects for providing bankers with specialized training. For example, the Financial Public Relations Association conducts a special summer school at Northwestern University, and the National Association of Bank Auditors and Comptrollers conducts a summer session at the University of Wisconsin. In addition, a number of state bankers' associations have organized helpful schools for junior bank employees. These several schools are serving a constructive purpose in American banking.

SUMMARY

There was almost complete unanimity among the supervisory agencies that the biggest problem and most glaring weakness of bank management today is that of successor management. Over 96 per cent expressed this view in their replies. In some cases the failure to develop responsibility in the supporting officers is deliberate, while in other instances this failure is caused by an inability or unwillingness to attempt to solve this difficult problem.

[2] The State Bankers' Associations of the following sixteen midwestern states: Arkansas, Colorado, Illinois, Indiana, Iowa, Kansas, Kentucky, Michigan, Minnesota, Missouri, Nebraska, North Dakota, Ohio, Oklahoma, South Dakota, Wisconsin.

[3] Catalogue, The School of Banking at the University of Wisconsin, 1955.

In addition, despite the fact that the banking industry long ago recognized the need for management training, little has been done to develop practical internal programs of personnel and executive development. A majority of the replies reported a failure of banks to train employees for their jobs.

To solve the problem of successor management, banks must attract able and alert young persons to the profession by offering them challenging responsibilities, attractive remuneration, and inspired leadership. This implies a willingness by management to train young people by delegating authority to them. Only in this way will the problem of successor management, the primary and most perplexing one facing bankers today, be solved.

SUGGESTED READINGS

AMERICAN MANAGEMENT ASSOCIATION, "Management Development: Key to Company Progress," *General Management Series*, No. 162, New York, American Management Association, 1953.

"An Executive Training Roundtable," *Banking*, Vol. 46, Nos. 2 and 3 (August and September 1953).

"Bringing Up the Boss," *Fortune*, Vol. 43, No. 6 (June 1951).

"The Crown Princes of Business," *Fortune*, Vol. 48, No. 4 (October 1953).

FREEMAN, GAYLORD A., JR., *The Selection, Training, and Development of Tomorrow's Executives: An Address to the Merchants' and Manufacturers' Association on October 25, 1954*, The First National Bank of Chicago.

MACE, MYLES L., *The Growth and Development of Executives*, Graduate School of Business Administration, Cambridge, Harvard University Press, 1950.

MEE, JOHN F., ed., *Personnel Handbook,* New York, The Ronald Press, 1951.

ODLE, HARRY V., "Developing Bank Executives," *Burroughs Clearing House,* Vol. 39, No. 6 (March 1955).

"Personnel—Some Current Problems," *The Journal of Business of the School of Business of the University of Chicago,* Vol. 28, No. 1 (January 1955).

PLANTY, EARL G. and FREESTON, J. THOMAS, *Developing Management Ability,* New York, The Ronald Press, 1954.

RIEGEL, JOHN W., *Executive Development: A Survey of Experience in Fifty American Corporations,* Ann Arbor, University of Michigan Press, 1952.

WORTHY, JAMES C., "Executive Personnel Development," *Advanced Management,* Vol. 18, No. 2 (February 1953).

————, "Planned Executive Development: The Experience of Sears, Roebuck and Company," *Practical Methods of Management Development,* Personnel Series No. 137, New York, American Management Association, 1951.

VIII

THE RESPONSIBILITIES
OF BANK DIRECTORS

The directors of American banks occupy a place of responsibility and power in the American economy. This responsibility, the policy direction of the banks of the nation, is ultimately charged to the board of directors. While it is true that the daily administration of the bank's operations is the duty and responsibility of the official staff, selected by the directors, the final responsibility rests in the hands of the directors. The stockholders and customers of a bank look to the directors for policy decisions that will provide the necessary safeguards for sound management. These are responsibilities not to be lightly accepted or casually discharged. This is of particular application to banks as distinguished from other types of corporations for the reason that "banks are generally considered to be quasi-public institutions, and hence their directors may be subjected to a somewhat higher degree of responsibility than directors of most other types of corporations."[1]

In the banks of the nation there are today over $200 billion

[1] C. W. Wilson, Jr., "Responsibilities of a Bank Director," *The Business Lawyer,* Vol. X, No. 3 (April 1955).

in deposits and more than $17 billion in capital funds. The savings deposits of $72 billion represent the savings of 68 million Americans, and the commercial deposits represent the cash reserves of practically every business and industrial enterprise in the entire country. In a broad sense the responsibility of directing 14,367 banks reaches into every home, every charitable, educational, and benevolent institution, and every business enterprise in every village, city, and state in the nation.

Every director, in a large measure, helps to instill the confidence of the public in a bank. He should be a man of excellent character and principles, and so far as possible a recognized leader in his own field of endeavor. An imposing roster of directors made up of well-known, highly esteemed citizens and financial leaders constitutes a reservoir of managerial talent that is a source of strength to the bank. Such a board of directors is also an added assurance to the depositors, borrowers, and stockholders that the affairs of the bank will be competently and intelligently administered. No bank can be successfully operated or serve its community well when the men who direct its policies or conduct its management place expediency before sound principles. If a director does not measure up to the highest standards of integrity and ability, his name may do the bank more harm than good. Not only may the bank's reputation be harmed but equally important, the bank may experience actual losses. In the list of qualifications of a good bank director, there are no substitutes for character, integrity, and ability.

On the other hand, no person is wise who permits himself to be elected a bank director unless he is confident that the management of the bank is competent and stands squarely for sound principles of banking. Otherwise he jeopardizes his good name and may even find himself liable for excessive loans or losses incurred through improper practices.

A bank director has many responsibilities. First there are those to the depositors. As mentioned above, a large percentage of the savings of the American people is placed in the care of our banks. The management and supervision of vast properties and funds place upon directors social and economic responsibilities of unusual magnitude. Every director must constantly be aware that the public has been invited to deposit its money with his bank on the assumption that it is managed with great care by competent men.

Second, the director obviously has an obligation to the stockholders who elect him. It is the director's responsibility to give stockholders a satisfactory return consistent with the sound and safe management of the bank.

To discharge these responsibilities the director must understand banking and the banking system. While the director obviously need not be familiar with all the day-to-day technical aspects of bank management and administration, he must be familiar with the basic banking functions and the role of the bank in the economic life of the community. In addition, he should have some concept of the relationship of his bank to the central banking system and the place of the central banking system in the economic life of the nation. Without such knowledge, his ability to contribute to the policy management decisions of the bank may be limited.

Because of the obligations and responsibilities of bank directors, the survey included several questions on this important subject. The national and state banking authorities were asked if they had observed a lack of interest on the part of the directors. Did they believe that bank directors were properly qualified by experience and ability? Based on their unusual experience in reviewing the activity of our 14,367 banks, the agencies were also asked whether they believed that the directors adequately supervise the banks' major policies.

About half of the forty-six replies stated that the directors do not take a satisfactory interest in the affairs of the bank. One, commenting at length on the subject wrote, "Not only is there a lack of interest on the part of many bank directors, but there is a failure on the part of directors to recognize fully their duties and responsibilities. We also find a real problem results from the continued re-election of men as directors who are of advanced age and who could be generally classified as retired. This is more of a problem in the smaller banks, because no one wants to hurt the oldster's feelings by asking him to resign or by not putting him up for re-election. In the case of a bank dominated by a very aggressive executive officer or by one who holds stock control, directors are prone to sit back and rubber-stamp management decisions." The report continued, "This may result from either lack of interest or inability to accomplish anything by showing interest.

"Generally speaking, bank directors are successful in their own lines of endeavor and so are capable, and probably it should be said that they are usually qualified by experience and ability. It is recognized, however, that few bank directors work in a bank. This is a handicap to them. In too many cases there is not adequate supervision of the bank's major policies by directors. In many cases such supervision is good but too often the board relies upon active management both to formulate policies and to carry them out."

Frequently expressed was the opinion that the management talents or abilities of the board are not fully utilized. To utilize such services, in the over-all policy decisions of the bank, may require effort on the part of the management to stimulate the interest of the directors in the operational activities of the bank.

One agency expressed it this way: "There is a surprising amount of untapped director interest in the banks. This observation is made on the strength of the evidence furnished examiners who have discussed an examination with the directors for the first time. It has been observed that most of the interest is lacking in the managing officer responsible for furnishing information to the directors in a form which will encourage their participation in management responsibility.

"While directors frequently lack bank administrative experience, they generally possess the business background which would be of material aid to the bank, if properly cultivated and encouraged," the same supervisor wrote. "There are many exceptions, of course, but there are few boards which do not possess two or three men besides the managing officers who have all the ability necessary to manage a bank. Whether this ability is utilized in coordinating management planning depends upon the controlling leadership of the bank. Many banks operate without any investment or administrative policy provided by the directors. As a consequence, the directors' supervision is far short of their legal and moral responsibility."

Another supervisory authority, commenting favorably and at length on directors, especially in rural banks, wrote, "When it comes to experience and ability of a country directorate, I can truthfully say that a majority of the country directors are qualified to pass upon local credits as these directors are usually born and reared in the area and have a great personal knowledge of the family background and moral integrity of the residents of their respective communities."

The same state supervisor mentioned in its reply that "while there was no banking law in their particular state requiring directors' examinations, many of the bylaws of country banks do require directors' examination of one form or another. It has been our considered judgment for many years," the agency suprisingly wrote, "that the so-called perfunctory examinations by directors are useless insofar as the over-all general protective features are concerned to the bank. We have been endeavoring with an educational program to get our correspondent city banks to make available to the country bankers personnel from the city bank's auditing department who might be used by the country banks in conjunction with the directors to conduct annual examinations. To the extent that we have been successful in this program, the results have been entirely satisfactory. We would say, however, that as an over-all picture, there is much to be desired in the way of improvement of adequate supervision by the directors of a rural bank's major policies."

By way of contrast with the previous comment, this same state agency wrote that "the availability of directors in rural sections also creates a problem in many instances. In the first instance, the available material for directors is limited, and in many cases, where there is suitable available material, those individuals are so busily engaged in their ordinary daily vocations that they are not disposed to sacrifice a sufficient amount of the time required to assume their full responsibilities as directors of banking institutions."

A careful analysis of the replies leads to the conclusion that there may be a failure on the part of the official management of the bank to generate director interest in the operation and condition of the bank. Either the executive officers of the bank dominate the board, or the information they furnish the board members is inadequate. In this situation, not only is the official staff at fault but the directors are failing to discharge their responsibility by not demanding the required information.

One supervisory authority emphasized this. "It is my observation," he wrote, "that regardless of a director's background, it is necessary to get him interested in his institution and its problems in order to develop him into a good director. Some bankers in our state are reluctant to take the directors into their confidence. Where this situation exists, I am convinced that there are unfortunate problems. It has been my policy to attempt to adjust these situations," wrote the supervisor, "and I believe that I have been successful in the results. I believe that on the whole there is adequate supervision of banks' major policies by directors. However, there are some bankers even in larger institutions who feel that it is their responsibility to supervise policies and who would like to operate independently of the board."

According to another reply, "the problem of encouraging directors really to direct the activities of a bank is a continuing one and complete compliance to supervisors' recommendations in this regard will probably never be achieved. Our department has recommended improvement of directors' activities in banks for many years, yet we still find that the recommendations must be repeated almost every time a new bank starts where the directors have had no previous experience."

One examiner, in evaluating the influence and role of directors, observed that "weak loans and poor operations spring largely from a disinterested, uninformed, and inexperienced directorate. In nearly every instance of banks having asset or other internal problems the root cause may be attributed to a board of directors who either willingly or negligently allow a 'one-man situation' to prevail."

This so-called "one-man bank," according to several banking authorities, is the result of the directors exercising too much authority. "Too often directors delegate authority to the executive officer and then fail to follow through. This leads frequently to the 'one-man' bank. Often one or two directors and the executive officer dominate the board. There is need for improvement in this area. Furthermore," the same report continued, "directors in numerous cases do not recognize their responsibilities and possible liabilities. There is a period of superannuation. Attendance is poor."

A weakness sometimes mentioned concerned the tendency for directors to pass down many of their responsibilities to the active management. One examiner commented, "One weakness, which we have seen present in both larger and smaller banks, is the heavy reliance by directors on their active management. Sometimes that management may be inept or it may be unethical. Yet the majority of the board members in some cases seem either unable or unwilling to recognize the frailties of the active management."

"With few exceptions," another supervisor wrote, "the directors are a success in business, but they delegate too much authority to their managing officers, and the managing officers really run the bank."

On the other hand, a few replies indicated that occasionally the directors will exercise too much authority, and that a director sometimes is the "one man." One comment pointed up the hazards of this situation. "In many individual cases, directors are retained on the board because of sentiment, their long service as directors, or the prestige of their names long after they have ceased to take an active interest in the bank's affairs because of various handicaps, senility, or removal from the community. It has been the policy of this department to urge banks to add younger and well qualified local business men to the board in cases where the directorates appear weak or appear to be dominated by one individual or group. Our experience indicates that there is adequate supervision of the bank's major policies by the directors in most instances, but some boards are dominated by one or more individuals who actually dictate not only the major policies but also operational procedures, by limiting the powers and authority of other officers so that they, in turn, are actually relegated to the status of senior clerks."

The following case history illustrates a situation where the directors demanded far too much detail from the official staff:

"The managing officer is, in my opinion, well qualified and

is doing his best. He has a good board of directors, and I met with them at the conclusion of our examination on Monday of this week. A firm of accountants have made their audit and recommended a program that is designed for a very much larger bank. As a result, the managing officer and his assistant were swamped with detail and with making reports to the directors. Sound operating and loan and investment policies had not received their due consideration and the minutes revealed that the directors spent more time on a $10 expense item than on a $10,000 loan or investment. This is not a problem bank in any sense, but a situation where the directors were requiring of the officers too much detail work that had little value."

A high degree of unity between the directors and the official staff, however, is necessary if a bank is to be well managed. To be successful, a bank must enjoy the complete confidence of the depositors, the stockholders, and the community that the bank serves. The solidarity and efficiency of any bank rests upon the cooperation among the board, the official staff, and the employees.

In many jurisdictions, one of the primary legal obligations of a bank director is to require an audit of the bank's records in order to deter and to detect any careless, extravagant, or fraudulent tendencies on the part of the personnel of the bank. The Comptroller of the Currency, for example, requires that a directors' committee, composed of board members who are not active officers, shall make an examination of the bank as often as possible, and in any event not less frequently than once a year. Directors cannot shield themselves from liability by pleading ignorance of a transaction in which they did not participate, when their ignorance is a result of their negligence and inattention.[2]

There are noted below some illustrations in which the negligence of the directors has been discussed by the courts. This is not intended as a comprehensive list but is cited merely for the purpose of indicating some specific examples.

First, failure to audit or examine the affairs and condition of the bank periodically, or failure to have the bank audited or examined.[3]

Second, allowing loans to be made without sufficient security.[4]

Third, failure to appoint a discount and loan committee, or an examining directors' committee, when required by the bylaws and/or the volume of the bank's business, or the failure to see that such committees function, if appointed.[5]

[2] "Liability of directors of a bank for losses to the bank, so far as any rule can be deducted from the various authorities and based on the facts of individual cases . . . can be stated as follows: Where the directors of a corporation are guilty of a breach or neglect of duty and the proximate result of such breach or neglect of duty is a loss to the bank, there may be a recovery from such directors." *Wallach* v. *Billings,* 277 Ill. 218,233 (1917), cert. denied, 244 U.S. 659.

[3] Mr. Justice Holmes referring to a Kansas Statute then in force: "As a matter of law there is nothing new in charging a party with knowledge of what it is his duty to know, in this case the insolvency of the bank, or with assent to deposits that he must expect while the bank's doors remain open. But the essential thing is that, whether in a roundabout or a perfectly natural way, the statute has said if you take the office you must take the consequences of knowledge whether you have it or not. In most contracts, men take the risk of events over which they have imperfect or no control. The acceptance of a directorship is as voluntary an act as a contract." *Ferry* v *Ramsey,* 277 U.S. 88, 95 (1928).

[4] *Medford Trust Co.* v *McKnight,* 197 N.E. 649 (1935); *Adams* v *Hendel,* 28 F. Supp. 317 (1939).

[5] *Prudential Trust Co.* v *Brown,* 171 N.E. 42 (1930); *Gamble* v *Brown,* 29 F2d 366 (1928), Certiorari Denied 279 U.S. 830.

Fourth, failure to direct the use of reasonable efforts to collect slow or doubtful assets.[6]

Fifth, permitting improvident expenditures in the conduct of the bank's business.[7]

Sixth, authorizing improvident investments.[8]

Seventh, failure to direct appropriate action to collect slow or doubtful loans due to the bank.[9]

Eighth, incurring damages resulting from a failure to charge off assets at the direction of the Comptroller of the Currency or supervising authority, or representing such assets to be good after such direction.[10]

[6] *Michelsen* v *Penney,* 135 F2d 409 (1943).

[7] *Ibid.*

[8] *Cockrill* v *Abeles,* 86 F 505, 512 (1898).

"But we cannot concede that the bank itself had the right to operate the mill, either in its own name or in that of an agent, and incur the risks which are necessarily incident to a business venture of that nature. The present case shows the hazards which attend such ventures, and the necessity, on grounds of public policy, of denying to national banks the right to become interested therein. The most liberal view which may be fairly taken of the implied powers of national banks would not sustain their right to engage directly in a manufacturing or business enterprise under any circumstances; but, even if the power in question should be conceded to exist under certain conditions, the present case was not one which warranted its exercise. The directors of the bank had no right to employ its funds in an attempt to operate the cotton mills for the bank's account, in the manner alleged in the bill, and such action on their part was unauthorized and wrongful."

See also *Medford Trust Co.* v *McKnight,* 197 N.E. 649 (1935).

[9] *Atherton* v *Anderson,* 99 F2d 883 (1938); *Litwin* v *Allen,* 25 N.Y.S. 667.

[10] *Thomas* v *Taylor,* 224 U.S. 73 (1912).

"They had notice from the Comptroller of the Currency that $194,000 of the items counted as assets of the bank were doubtful and should be collected or charged off. This was a direct warning to them," as the trial court said, "by the bank examiner and Comptroller that assets to nearly twice the amount of the capital stock were considered doubtful. They, notwithstanding, represented the assets to be good. Such disregard of the direction of the officers appointed by the law to examine the affairs of the bank is a violation of the law. Their directions must be observed. Their function and authority cannot be preserved otherwise and be exercised to save the banks from disaster and the public who deal with them and support them from deception."

Ninth, allowing improvident overdrafts.[11]

Tenth, losses resulting from failure to require a proper bond from officers and employees of the bank.[12]

Eleventh, permitting control by incompetent officials.[13]

In addition, Federal and State statutes have provisions setting forth certain duties and liabilities of directors. For example, as to national banks, Section 5239 of the United States Revised Statutes (12 U. S. C. 93) provides that if any director knowingly violates, or knowingly permits any officer or agent of the bank to violate, any provision of the National Bank Act, the director will be personally liable for all damages which the bank or any stockholders or any other person may sustain as a result of such violation. Section 22 (F) of the Federal Reserve Act (12 U. S. C. 503) contains a similar provision applicable to directors of all member banks. There are provisions in respect to excessive loans and investments, false reports to the Comptroller of the Currency, improper dividends, interest on deposits, and loans to officers.

Many of the statutes also subject the directors to certain criminal liabilities. Briefly, the National Bank Act provides for criminal liabilities for embezzlement and misapplication of funds, for making false entries, for certifying checks where there are insufficient funds, for making political contributions from bank funds, and for loaning trust funds to officers or employees of the bank. The F.D.I.C. Act subjects officers or directors of any bank insured by the F.D.I.C. to a fine of not more than $5000 or imprisonment for not more

---

[11] *Gamble* v *Brown,* 29 F2d 366 (1928); *McCormick* v *King,* 241 F. 737 (1917).

[12] *Gamble* v *Brown,* 29 F2d 366 (1928).

[13] *Bowerman* v *Hammer,* 250 U.S. 504 (1919).

than one year, or both, for receiving a fee or gift from any person or corporation in connection with procuring a loan for such person or corporation from the bank.

Fortunately, most directors are deeply dedicated to their responsibilities and opportunities, and have an intense desire to strengthen their banks.

SUMMARY

A summary of the views on the subject of bank directors and their responsibilities indicates that:

First, about half of the agencies replying to the questionnaire were of the opinion that directors do not take a satisfactory interest in the affairs of the bank.

Second, this lack of interest is often the result of a failure on the part of management to generate director interest in the activities of the bank.

Third, most bank directors are exceptionally capable businessmen whose managerial abilities and talents can be an invaluable asset to their bank. Whether these abilities are tapped and utilized in coordinated management planning depends upon the leadership within the bank.

SUGGESTED READINGS

"Today's Directors Keep Informed," *Banking,* Vol. 45, No. 12 (June 1953).

LYON, WILLIAM A., "The Responsibilities and Opportunities of Bank Directors," *Banking,* Vol. 44, No. 9 (March 1952).

McDAVITT, CLARENCE G., JR., *If You're a Bank Director,* Cambridge, Banker's Publishing Company, 1950.

OFFICE OF THE COMPTROLLER OF THE CURRENCY, *Duties and Liabilities of Directors of National Banks;* Treasury Department, Washington.

PRENTICE-HALL, *Directors' and Officers' Encyclopedic Manual,* New York, Prentice-Hall, Inc., 1955.

WILSON, C. W., JR., "Responsibilities of a Bank Director," *The Business Lawyer,* Vol. X, No. 3 (April 1955).

WRIGHT, MILTON, "The Bank's Directors," *Banking,* New York, 1942.

IX

A BANK'S ADVERTISING
AND PUBLIC RELATIONS PROGRAM

A BANK'S advertising and public relations program, although a significant responsibility of management, was not included in the survey questionnaire for a number of reasons. First, it is not a matter that comes within the direct purview of the examining authorities. Second, there is no widely accepted standard or norm with which to make a comparison. As a consequence, it was felt that it would be unfair to ask the examining authorities to evaluate the public relations and advertising programs of banks under their jurisdiction.

To be effective a bank's advertising and public relations program must be clearly defined and rooted in reality. To do this, management must with candor recognize not only where banking has succeeded but also where it has failed of accomplishment. Such a review and appraisal may sometimes require bankers to abandon old concepts and experiment with new methods.

There are some who have said that a public relations program is necessary because of the competition banks are experiencing from other institutions and organizations. If this be the primary motivating force, the public relations program is not likely to be adequate or to meet its responsibilities. The real objectives of a bank's advertising and public relations program require a broader, more constructive view.

The subject of advertising and public relations is one in which all bankers have a common interest. If our advertising and public relations programs are to be effective, we must have a clear and precise understanding of our objectives and of the steps required to attain them.

TWO MAJOR RESPONSIBILITIES

At the risk of oversimplifying the subject, we may say that there are two major responsibilities in the broad field of advertising and public relations. The first relates to the over-all planning of the advertising and the advertising budget; analysis of markets, evaluation and selection of advertising media, preparation of copy, knowledge of type, paper stock, and color, and an understanding of all those specialized techniques which distinguish the groping amateur from the confident professional who carries on his activities with assurance and competence.

In discharging these responsibilities, at least one person in every bank is confronted with some highly technical decisions. For example, should he use Goudy Heavyface Italic or Ultra Bodoni Italic as the type face in the advertising? Would a deckle edge on a booklet make it a little more impressive? Are six advertisements of one page each better than twelve of one-half page? Which advertising media reach a market most effectively? Will his bank pioneer in its art work, or accept the more traditional? Is the copy too long or too short?

Should he follow the senior officer's idea of layout or an advertising agency's judgment? How should he deal with the superior officer who lets an advertising campaign gather dust on the top of his desk for three months? What does he do when an officer rewrites vigorous copy so it comes out as meaningless generalities? These are all part of the day's work, or perhaps one should say "headaches," for the bank officer who handles the advertising and public relations.

Then there are similar practical problems which are related to publicity. How can the first paragraph of a news release be written so it gets used? Should the story break in the morning or afternoon newspapers? How can he prepare good news stories instead of releases which merely advertise his own institution? Perhaps we may paraphrase an old quotation by saying that in sending out publicity releases without real news in them one may fool some of the publications all of the time, and all of the publications some of the time, but one never fools all the publications all the time.

The first responsibility then is to handle efficiently and intelligently the broad scope of activities of which we have presented here only the most concise summary. In general, it may be said that all types of financial institutions are performing these functions with increasing ability and competence. In fact, we may sometimes even have a lingering regret that our competitors have become so intelligent and able in preparing their advertising and promoting their services.

The second major responsibility in our advertising and public relations program falls squarely on the shoulders of the senior management. It is the responsibility of the senior officials to establish and follow policies that will practically and effectively implement these programs. It is their responsibility to take those concrete and definite steps that will actually give the advertising and publicity reality. In discharging this responsibility, we have been less farsighted and less competent than we have been in advancing the technical skills of advertising and publicity.

The policies of the senior management may either make or break the advertising and public relations program of an institution. They may make it effective or they may seriously impair its value. The sound growth and the continued progress of all financial institutions are dependent upon the proper discharge of these duties. Perhaps we can illustrate the significance of this responsibility by asking a few questions.

Are the services of the institution constantly under critical analysis to see whether the public is receiving the comprehensive service which the institution advertises and to which the public is entitled? It is one thing to be certain that the telephone operators and the employees answer telephones promptly and courteously. It is another matter to be certain that a financial institution is steadily increasing its capital structure so it can take care of growing businesses and not stifle the economic development of its community and the well-being of its people.

It is one thing to advertise friendly and courteous service in broad generalities with words that have been worn thin by constant usage. It is another matter aggressively to seek opportunities in the community to make loans where they should be made, and to assume sound credit risks instead of avoiding them.

It is one thing to be sure that tellers greet customers pleasantly and to remember that the Jones Grocery Store is one of the bank's oldest and most valued customers. It is another matter for officers to speak out courageously on controversial economic, monetary, and fiscal problems, and legislation that vitally affect the business life of the Jones Grocery Store.

It is not enough merely to accept the minor readjustments that progress and our competitors force upon us. It takes courage and imagination to analyze objectively an entire bank or other financial institution and find that a whole new department will have to be organized if the community is to get proper service. Perhaps a bank needs a consumer credit department, much better auditing and accounting controls, an enlargement of its credit department, a trust department, a foreign department. Perhaps an entire new safe deposit unit needs to be installed. Perhaps the whole physical layout of a bank needs to be changed at considerable expense and inconvenience. Perhaps the entire personnel policy needs to be re-examined if the institution is to make the most effective use of its employees and officers and attract to it the ablest young men and women in the community. It is easy to postpone such important decisions and retard an institution and the community it serves. But these are policy decisions that have a far reaching impact on advertising and public relations problems. These are problems requiring decisions which may involve substantial expenditures, and they are major factors in determining whether an advertising and public relations program succeeds or fails.

Consider another aspect of this responsibility of the senior management. Are the lines of authority among officials of the institution clearly drawn? Do officers have proper authority to make commitments specifically delegated to them, or are decisions delayed and customers kept waiting? Under any competent executive training program it is imperative that officers be given fixed, definite authority in accordance with their positions. Advertising that urges customers to present their financial problems to officers who do not have clear and specific authority to make prompt decisions will soon be without acceptance in the business community.

Moreover, if an officer fully understands the extent to which he can with assurance commit his institution, the customer has the satisfaction of presenting his problem and getting an answer. The institution is also assured of the steady growth in executive responsibility of its officers. To be known as an institution where one's financial problems are understood and where prompt decisions are given is an asset of inestimable value in the advertising and public relations program.

To earn this reputation, another imperative step is a thorough program of executive training. Before officers are placed in positions to make major decisions, they must have had careful and conscientious training. For example, in commercial banking it means that a lending officer must have a thorough knowledge of the financial problems of the businesses and industries to which he commits the depositors' funds. If his bank is in an agricultural community, he needs to study all the intricate problems of that complex industry. The farm community has a right to expect such leadership from him. His bank may well become the recognized center for agricultural information and advice in the community.

Some banks have attained that distinction. That is one way to make public relations practical and effective. If you could multiply one such bank by fifteen thousand banks thoroughly informed regarding industry after industry, we would take gigantic strides in building the prestige of American banking. And we would enable bank advertising and public relations to reach new levels of usefulness and achievement.

The banker should know the economic trends in every industry with which he deals. He needs to understand production and sales problems, costs, inventory turnover, competition, and a multitude of other problems related to the financial needs of each industry he finances. Armed with this knowledge and with the authority to make decisions, he will analyze with the highest degree of intelligence the customers' balance sheets, profit and loss statements, and budgets. He will give life and vigor to the bank's advertising and public relations. The community will find a bank that is friendly and courteous, as we have paid a good many advertising dollars to tell them. But even more important, the community will find a bank that is intelligent. We must never forget that friendliness may walk hand in hand with ignorance as well as with intelligence; and when it does, an advertising and public relations program loses its power and force.

ARTICULATE LEADERSHIP

There is still another aspect of this second responsibility which in some respects transcends all others in its importance. We not only need to understand the monetary, fiscal, industrial and economic problems that relate to the financial institutions of our communities, but we also need to have the courage to give articulate and aggressive leadership to the solution of these problems. Stated bluntly, we need to speak boldly and publicly on local, state, and national problems that affect our institutions and our communities. We can never be accused of having been too articulate in the past.

Our institutions occupy positions of unusual importance in the economy of the nation. They are closely related to all industries, all government and public bodies, and to the financial welfare of every person in the nation. In our institutions we deal each day with the hopes and fortunes and lives of millions of men and women. The stewardship for much of the nation's wealth is entrusted to us. Good financial leadership, as we have stated, requires that we be thoroughly informed regarding major economic, monetary, industrial, and fiscal problems. If our institutions are well-informed economic and financial centers, surely we have an obligation to express our views on these matters clearly and positively. If we are not to state our convictions on these problems which are directly related to the welfare of our institutions and our customers, employees, and stockholders, whose responsibility is it to speak? Is it the mark of financial leadership to wait until others express their views in public, in the press, and in legislation, and then offer only criticism of those views? If we are not prepared for such leadership, it inevitably passes to other hands. We have too often surrendered our leadership to others who spoke with far less authority and far less right. Consequently, our reluctance to state our views on major issues publicly has often lessened the effectiveness of our advertising and publicity. We criticize. We deplore. But we too seldom lead. And yet our place in the nation's economy, our experience, and our training qualify us for leadership. Surely we have some responsibility for informing our communities of what we believe are sound monetary, fiscal, and economic policies. In any community, that responsibility unquestionably rests upon the leaders of its financial institutions.

In our advertising we tell the people of our competence in handling financial problems, and of our understanding of the problems of American industry. But when such problems are discussed publicly and in legislation, we are strangely silent. One is hesitant to believe we are so uninformed or have such little confidence in what we so freely state in our advertising and publicity regarding our own competence.

However, we must not underestimate what leadership of this character will require. It means that we shall have to study monetary, economic, industrial, and fiscal problems in a far more thorough manner than we ever have done in the past. One does not become an authority on the nation's fiscal and monetary problems by a casual reading of the day's headlines. One does not become an authority on the financial problems and the trends in great industries by a study of the Dow-Jones averages. In the complicated economy in which we now operate our institutions, we need a higher level of management ability than has ever been required in the past. We need management that thoroughly understands the great industries it finances; management that can express intelligent views regarding difficult national fiscal and monetary problems; management that is aware of all the intricate functions and operations of the Federal Reserve System. That kind of management has something more than friendliness, courtesy, and a good telephone personality, important as those qualities are. That kind of management has something more than a shallow knowledge of the day's routine. And it is only that kind of management which can give strength and character and effectiveness to our advertising and public relations.

We shall find as we express our views publicly that they will be carefully analyzed, and sometimes they will be strongly criticized. But it is certain that the leadership of our financial institutions will gain increased esteem if we discharge these responsibilities more adequately. And our advertising and public relations will be raised to new levels of achievement.

CONCLUSION

In connection with our first responsibility, we need constantly to improve our knowledge of the techniques and procedures of advertising and public relations. We have made great progress in this direction, and through research, experience, and study we are certain to increase further the effectiveness of all financial advertising and public relations.

But in connection with the second responsibility relating to the duties of senior management as they affect advertising and public relations, we have much to accomplish. It is the duty of the officer who is responsible for the bank's advertising and public relations to give the senior officers information, ideas, and assistance that will help them to discharge their particular responsibilities for the success of advertising and public relations.

There is one aspect of this second responsibility where the advertising and public relations officer could be greatly helpful, and where he may not have placed sufficient emphasis in the past. He thoughtfully works out the most complete advertising campagins and publicity releases, but he assumes that the senior management is equally informed regarding his program and what he is trying to accomplish. He may sometimes forget that the senior management has many problems and a number of departments, all of which urgently press for attention. He should be certain that the management is thoroughly informed regarding his plans and his objectives so that the management itself may discharge its important responsibility effectively in relation to the entire public relations program.

To the extent, then, that management meets the challenges we have outlined, becomes more competent and better informed, and courageously expresses its views as it takes the leadership in dealing with monetary, economic, industrial, and fiscal problems—to that extent the advertising and public relations of all financial institutions will take new and major forward strides.

SUGGESTED READINGS

AMERICAN BANKERS ASSOCIATION, Public Relations Council, *Public Relations, Opportunities and Tools, for A.B.A. Members,* New York, American Bankers Association, 1953.

BAUS, HERBERT M., *Public Relations at Work,* New York, Harper & Brothers, 1948.

BURNETT, VERNE, *You and Your Public,* New York, Harper & Brothers, 1947.

CUTLIP, SCOTT M. and CENTER, ALLEN H., *Effective Public Relations: Pathways to Public Favor,* New York, Prentice-Hall, Inc., 1952.

DUNN, WILLIAM T., *Practical Public Relations in Banking,* Cambridge, The Bankers Publishing Company, 1950.

FINANCIAL PUBLIC RELATIONS ASSOCIATION, *Proceedings of Annual Conventions*, Various Years.

FITZGERALD, STEPHEN E., *Communicating Ideas to the Public*, New York, Funk & Wagnalls Company in association with *Modern Industry*, 1950.

GRAS, N. S. B., *Business and Capitalism; An Introduction to Business History*, New York, F. S. Crofts & Co., 1939.

————, "Shifts in Public Relations," *Bulletin of the Business Historical Society*, Baker Library, Soldiers Field, Boston, Vol. 19, No. 4 (October 1945).

GRISWOLD, GLENN and GRISWOLD, DENNY, *Your Public Relations*, New York, Funk & Wagnalls Company in association with *Modern Industry*, 1948.

HARLOW, REX F. and BLACK, MARVIN M., *Practical Public Relations*, New York, Harper & Brothers, 1947.

HETTINGER, HERMAN S., *Financial Public Relations: For the Business Corporation*, New York, Harper & Brothers, 1954.

ILG, RAY A., *Public Relations for Banks*, New York, Harper & Brothers, 1937.

LESLY, PHILIP, *Public Relations Handbook*, New York, Prentice-Hall, Inc., 1950.

PIMLOTT, J. A. R., *Public Relations and American Democracy*, Princeton, Princeton University Press, 1951.

PRINTERS' INK EDITORS AND CONTRIBUTORS, *Public Relations Idea Books*, New York, Printers' Ink Publishing Company, 1953.

WEDDING, NUGENT, "Public Relations in Business," *University of Illinois Bulletin (Bureau of Economic and Business Research, Bulletin Series No. 71)*, Vol. 47, No. 79 (July 1950).

WHYTE, WILLIAM H., JR., and the editors of *Fortune, Is Anybody Listening? How and Why U.S. Business Fumbles When It Talks with Human Beings*, New York, Simon & Schuster, Inc., 1952.

WRIGHT, J. HANDLY and CHRISTIAN, BYRON H., *Public Relations in Management*, New York, McGraw-Hill Book Company, Inc., 1949.

X

SUMMARY OF THE SURVEY

AT THE outset of this book it was asserted that the one responsibility of the banker which transcends every other banking obligation is the responsibility to manage his bank with the highest degree of competency, so that the safety of the bank's deposits is assured.

This final chapter is intended to give the reader in outline arrangement a quick summary of the conclusions of the forty-six supervisory agencies who responded to the questionnaire on bank management.

THE BANK LOAN PORTFOLIO

1. Failure to require a definite repayment plan is the most frequent cause of losses on loans.

2. Loans are not adequately policed.

3. Too much reliance is placed on collateral security instead of on the borrower's ability to repay out of earnings.

4. Prompt and efficient collection measures are not instituted soon enough, or are too lenient.

5. An excellent risk ten years ago is not necessarily a good risk today.

6. Excellent character is not enough to protect the bank's assets.

7. Loans made on a "good neighbor" basis are no substitute for sound collateral values.

8. Marginal customers often are permitted to pyramid loans.

9. Liberalized loan standards frequently follow low interest rates.

10. A surprising number of losses result from the bank's having no claim against the borrower because of inadequate legal provision in the loan agreement.

11. Lack of loan diversification by industry frequently causes loan losses.

12. The technical knowledge and operational experience of lending officers was considered adequate, but an increased awareness of general economic conditions would be desirable.

THE CREDIT FILES OF THE BANK

1. Credit files are frequently not kept current.

2. Important conferences with the borrower are not always noted in the credit file.

3. The loaning officer's appraisal of the borrower's financial condition occasionally is not recorded.

4. Credit files are often incomplete as a result of a failure to ask the borrower for needed information, or because the lending officers keep credit information "in their heads" instead of in a credit file.

5. Lending officers sometimes rely too heavily on their personal acquaintance with the borrowers.

6. Personal interviews are an important source of credit information.

7. Many examiners noted that there is a failure to act

promptly on information about a borrower's changing circumstances as it becomes available.

8. There is a failure thoroughly to investigate the personal life of the borrower for extravagant living habits.

THE BANK BOND PORTFOLIO

1. Generally the bond portfolios of the banks of the United States are reasonably well managed.

2. The large metropolitan banks have specially trained staffs managing their portfolios.

3. Some smaller banks have a real and practical problem of bond portfolio management because of personnel limitations.

4. There is a tendency to reach for yields.

5. Proper maturity selection often is ignored.

6. Bankers should carefully study and systematically review deposit fluctuations and appropriately arrange bond maturity schedules.

7. The responsibility of the management of the bond account of the bank should be centralized.

8. Investment policy should be clearly defined.

CAPITAL, SURPLUS AND RESERVES

1. Earnings in most banks are considered adequate to build strong capital, surplus, and reserve accounts.

2. The earnings of some banks however are insufficient because of relatively low yields on loans and investments combined with high tax rates.

3. Programs for building capital, surplus, and reserve accounts frequently are not clearly and definitely outlined.

4. Dividend disbursements at times interfere with capital expansion programs.

5. Many banks have ill-advised programs in regard to the payment of interest on time and savings deposits.

6. Progress is being made in strengthening the capital accounts of banks.

ACCOUNTING, INTERNAL CONTROL, AND TAXES

1. Accounting and internal control deficiencies are more serious in the small or medium sized banks.

2. In general, banks with resources of approximately $10 million or more should have full-time auditors.

3. Banks without adequate auditing programs have often been slow to recognize the value of an audit by a firm of public accountants as a supplement to the internal audit system. There is a growing interest in some type of audit program.

4. When internal audit programs are inadequate or non-existent, an outside auditing firm should be retained.

5. The primary obstacle to adequate audit programs is insufficient personnel.

6. Bankers are tax conscious, and keep themselves reasonably well informed on tax matters.

7. Many managements are not convinced of the necessity of adequate audit reports to the directors.

8. The responsibility for adequate internal controls rests squarely on the management of the bank.

PERSONNEL TRAINING AND SUCCESSOR MANAGEMENT

1. Successor management is the biggest problem confronting bank management today.

2. Some managements are reluctant to give responsibility to younger officers.

3. Management deficiencies are most frequently prevalent in "one-man" banks.

4. Executive officers and directors do not give sufficient attention to the problem of successor management.

5. Challenging and stimulating responsibilities must be offered to promising young persons if the problem of successor management is to be solved.

6. Bank salaries have improved.

7. The "prestige" formerly associated with employment in the banking field is no longer a consideration to many young people in the selection of banking as a career.

8. Little has been done to develop practical internal programs of personnel and executive development.

9. Formal education and training is becoming increasingly significant.

THE RESPONSIBILITIES OF BANK DIRECTORS

1. Many directors do not take a satisfactory interest in the affairs of their banks.

2. Bank directors do not adequately supervise bank policies.

3. Directors are not fully aware of their duties and responsibilities.

4. Directors generally possess the business background which would be of material aid to the bank.

5. Banks in rural areas not infrequently have difficulty replacing retiring directors.

6. The management of the bank at times fails to generate director interest in the operation of the bank.

7. Executive officers of the bank occasionally dominate the board too much.

8. In some banks, there is a tendency for directors to pass down too many of their responsibilities to the active management.

9. Some directors exercise too much authority.

10. One of the primary legal obligations of a bank director is to require an audit of the bank's records.

APPENDIX A

QUESTIONNAIRE SENT TO ALL THE NATIONAL AND STATE BANKING AUTHORITIES

SURVEY OF BANK MANAGEMENT

Based on your broad experience, would you give your views regarding bank management generally under the headings indicated below, giving such remarks as you believe would be helpful in a practical discussion of this subject with bankers. Any comments you wish to make relative to any of the items below will be appreciated. The space provided for each answer may not be sufficient. Please give additional remarks and illustrations on separate sheets. The source of the comments received will be completely confidential.

1. Loan portfolio
    A. What weaknesses in lending do you find most often?
        a. Are the officers poorly qualified and trained as loaning officers?
        b. Poor credit files?
        c. Failure to get financial statements?
        d. Ignorance of the customer's business?
        e. Other weaknesses?
    B. What are the most frequent causes of losses on loans?
        a. Lack of information?
        b. Poor judgment in extending credit?
        c. Other causes?
2. Bond portfolio
    A. What weaknesses in handling the bond account do you find most often?

    a. Poor spacing of maturities?

    b. No definite centralized responsibility for the bond account?

    c. Reaching for yields?

    d. Lack of adequate knowledge of the whole subject of bonds?

3. Capital, Surplus, Reserves, and Earnings

    A. Are earnings adequate to build strong capital and surplus accounts?

    B. Is there a satisfactory program for building capital, surplus, and reserves?

    C. Is there a lack of adequate reserves for losses and contingencies?

    D. Is there a failure to make proper charges for services?

4. Accounting and Auditing

    A. Are the accounting systems generally poor?

    B. Is there failure to have a bank auditor or an outside auditing firm?

    C. Is the knowledge of tax problems poor?

    D. Are reports to management and directors adequate?

    E. Is the insurance sufficient to cover possible losses?

5. Officers and Employees

    A. Is there failure to plan for continuing top management?

    B. Is there failure to train employees for their jobs?

    C. Are salaries adequate for officers?

    D. Are salaries adequate for employees?

6. Directors

    A. Is there a lack of interest on the part of the directors?

    B. Are the directors properly qualified by experience and ability?

    C. Is there adequate supervision of the bank's major policies by directors?

Any actual illustrations, changing names so that the identity of the bank is in no way revealed, would be greatly appreciated.

APPENDIX B

NATIONAL AND STATE BANKING AUTHORITIES

William McChesney Martin, Jr.
Chairman, Board of Governors
Federal Reserve System
Washington, D. C.

Ray M. Gidney
Comptroller of the Currency
Treasury Department
Washington, D. C.

H. Earl Cook, Chairman
Federal Deposit Insurance Corporation
Washington, D. C.

ALABAMA: Joe H. Williams, Superintendent of Banks, Montgomery.

ARIZONA: David O. Saunders, Superintendent of Banks, Phoenix.

ARKANSAS: A. R. Merritt, Bank Commissioner, Little Rock.

CALIFORNIA: Maurice C. Sparling, Superintendent of Banks, San Francisco.

COLORADO: DeWitt McNutt, Chief Deputy and Acting State Bank Commissioner, Denver.

CONNECTICUT: Lynwood K. Elmore, Bank Commissioner, Hartford.

DELAWARE: Randolph Hughes, State Bank Commissioner, Dover.

FLORIDA: Clarence M. Gay, State Commissioner of Banking, Tallahassee.

GEORGIA: Augustus P. Persons, Superintendent of Banks, Atlanta.

HAWAII: W. Lloyd Lederer, Deputy Bank Examiner, Honolulu.

IDAHO: R. U. Spaulding, Commissioner of Finance, Boise.

ILLINOIS: Orville Hodge, Auditor of Public Accounts, Springfield.

INDIANA: E. E. MacDonald, Supervisor of Banks, Indianapolis.

Iowa: Newton P. Black, Superintendent of Banks, Des Moines.

Kansas: Elmer T. Beck, Bank Commissioner, Topeka.

Kentucky: Henry H. Carter, Commissioner of Banking, Frankfort.

Louisiana: Edward F. Follett, State Bank Commissioner, Baton Rouge.

Maine: Homer E. Robinson, Bank Commissioner, Augusta.

Maryland: William H. Kirkwood, Jr., Bank Commissioner, Baltimore.

Massachusetts: Timothy J. Donovan, Commissioner of Banks, Boston.

Michigan: Maurice C. Eveland, Bank Commissioner, Lansing.

Minnesota: Charles M. Wenzel, Commissioner of Banks, St. Paul.

Mississippi: C. T. Johnson, State Comptroller, Jackson.

Missouri: J. A. Rouveyrol, Commissioner of Finance, Jefferson City.

Montana: R. E. Towle, Superintendent of Banks, Helena.

Nebraska: J. Floyd McLain, Director of Banking, Lincoln.

Nevada: Grant L. Robison, Superintendent of Banks, Carson City.

New Hampshire: Winfield J. Phillips, Bank Commissioner, Concord.

New Jersey: Warren N. Gaffney, Commissioner of Banking and Insurance, Trenton.

New Mexico: Alfred W. Kaune, State Bank Examiner, Santa Fe.

New York: William A. Lyon, Superintendent of Banks, New York.

North Carolina: William W. Jones, Commissioner of Banks, Raleigh.

North Dakota: John A. Graham, State Examiner, Bismarck.

Ohio: Paul Hinkle, Superintendent of Banks, Columbus.

Oklahoma: O. B. Mothersead, State Bank Commissioner, Oklahoma City.

Oregon: A. A. Rogers, Superintendent of Banks, Salem.

Pennsylvania: L. Merle Campbell, Secretary of Banking, Harrisburg.

Puerto Rico: S. L. Descartes, Treasurer, San Juan.

Rhode Island: Alexander Chmielewski, Bank Commissioner, Providence.

SOUTH CAROLINA: C. V. Pierce, Chief Bank Examiner, Columbia.

SOUTH DAKOTA: Roy H. Fenner, Superintendent of Banks, Pierre.

TENNESSEE: Homer B. Clarke, Superintendent of Banks, Nashville.

TEXAS: J. M. Falkner, Bank Commissioner, Austin.

UTAH: Louis S. Leatham, Bank Commissioner, Salt Lake City.

VERMONT: Alexander Miller, Commissioner of Banking and Insurance, Montpelier.

VIRGINIA: Logan R. Ritchie, Commissioner of Banking, Richmond.

WASHINGTON: Ray D. Carrell, Supervisor of Banking, Olympia.

WEST VIRGINIA: John H. Hoffman, Commissioner of Banking, Charleston.

WISCONSIN: Guerdon M. Matthews, Commissioner of Banks, Madison.

WYOMING: Norris E. Hartwell, State Bank Examiner, Cheyenne.